Playing Sociology

STUDIES IN VIOLENCE, MIMESIS, AND CULTURE

SERIES EDITOR
William A. Johnsen

The Studies in Violence, Mimesis, and Culture Series examines issues related to the nexus of violence and religion in the genesis and maintenance of culture. It furthers the agenda of the Colloquium on Violence and Religion, an international association that draws inspiration from René Girard's mimetic hypothesis on the relationship between violence and religion, elaborated in a stunning series of books he has written over the last forty years. Readers interested in this area of research can also look to the association's journal, *Contagion: Journal of Violence, Mimesis, and Culture*.

ADVISORY BOARD

René Girard[†], *Stanford University*
Andrew McKenna, *Loyola University of Chicago*

Raymund Schwager[†], *University of Innsbruck*
James Williams, *Syracuse University*

EDITORIAL BOARD

Rebecca Adams, *Independent Scholar*
Jeremiah L. Alberg, *International Christian University, Tokyo, Japan*
Mark Anspach, *École des Hautes Études en Sciences Sociales, Paris*
Pierpaolo Antonello, *University of Cambridge*
Ann Astell, *University of Notre Dame*
Cesáreo Bandera, *University of North Carolina*
Maria Stella Barberi, *Università di Messina*
Alexei Bodrov, *St. Andrew's Biblical Theological Institute, Moscow*
João Cezar de Castro Rocha, *Universidade do Estado do Rio de Janeiro*
Benoît Chantre, *L'Association Recherches Mimétiques*
Diana Culbertson, *Kent State University*
Paul Dumouchel, *Ritsumeikan University*
Jean-Pierre Dupuy, *Stanford University, École Polytechnique*
Giuseppe Fornari, *Università degli studi di Verona*
Eric Gans, *University of California, Los Angeles*

Sandor Goodhart, *Purdue University*
Robert Hamerton-Kelly[†], *Stanford University*
Hans Jensen, *Aarhus University, Denmark*
Mark Juergensmeyer, *University of California, Santa Barbara*
Cheryl Kirk-Duggan, *Shaw University*
Michael Kirwan, SJ, *Heythrop College, University of London*
Paisley Livingston, *Lingnan University, Hong Kong*
Charles Mabee, *Ecumenical Theological Seminary, Detroit*
Józef Niewiadomski, *Universität Innsbruck*
Wolfgang Palaver, *Universität Innsbruck*
Ángel Jorge Barahona Plaza, *Universidad Francisco de Vitoria*
Martha Reineke, *University of Northern Iowa*
Tobin Siebers[†], *University of Michigan*
Thee Smith, *Emory University*
Mark Wallace, *Swarthmore College*
Eugene Webb, *University of Washington*

Playing Sociology

**Theory and Games for Coping
with Mimetic Crisis and Social Conflict**

Martino Doni and Stefano Tomelleri

Michigan State University Press · *East Lansing*

Copyright © 2024 by Martino Doni and Stefano Tomelleri

Michigan State University Press
East Lansing, Michigan 48823-5245

LIBRARY OF CONGRESS CATALOGING-IN-PUBLICATION DATA
Names: Doni, Martino, author. | Tomelleri, Stefano, 1971– author.
Title: Playing sociology : theory and games for coping with mimetic crisis and social conflict /
Martino Doni and Stefano Tomelleri.
Description: East Lansing : Michigan State University Press, [2024] |
Series: Studies in violence, mimesis, and culture |
Includes bibliographical references and index.
Identifiers: LCCN 2023057273 | ISBN 9781611864977 (paperback) |
ISBN 9781609177669 | ISBN 9781628955279
Subjects: LCSH: Sociology—Study and teaching. |
Play—Social aspects. | Play—Psychological aspects.
Classification: LCC HM571 .D65 2024 | DDC 301.072—dc23/eng/20240112
LC record available at https://lccn.loc.gov/2023057273

Cover design by David Drummond, Salamander Design, www.salamanderhill.com.
Cover art: Children play blind man's bluff, iStock.

Visit Michigan State University Press at *msupress.org*

Contents

vii	INTRODUCTION
1	CHAPTER 1. Rules Are Needed to Play
15	CHAPTER 2. Envy and Paranoia: The Traps of Play
39	CHAPTER 3. Sympathy for Play
55	CHAPTER 4. Sociological Games
65	CHAPTER 5. Tribe: The Leader and the Sacrifice
79	CHAPTER 6. Thermopylae: Playing at War
93	CHAPTER 7. Polis: Participation and Skills
107	CHAPTER 8. Collapse: Before It's Too Late
125	CHAPTER 9. Zombies: Every Ending Is a Beginning
139	CHAPTER 10. Playing Sociology: Notes on Method and Analysis
151	REFERENCES

Introduction

IN THIS BOOK, WE WILL DESCRIBE A UNIVERSALLY WIDESPREAD HUMAN practice: play. We will do so from a particular point of view, that of sociology. It is not taken for granted that there is or can be such a point of view. Traditionally, play has been discussed, observed, explained, and almost vivisected by sciences far fiercer than sociology: sciences that, on their side, can boast not only a specific pedigree but also an apparatus of possible applications that sociology cannot but contemplate with envy from a certain distance. Human sciences such as dynamic psychology and cultural anthropology, for example, seem to be the most qualified to say the first and last word about play as a human phenomenon. Sociology, if anything, could add some statistical trappings or, at most, some generalizations, as is peculiar to it, that would remove distinctions, different perspectives, or cultural and individual characteristics. In doing so, sociology would find its own respectable niche, however much its apparent clumsy simplifications would risk sending the more intransigent and less tolerant representatives of other disciplines into a rage, who would look with a certain contempt upon the attempts and errors of those who seek to isolate a general tendency, a systemic and non-idiosyncratic relationship between individuals and the world they are a part of.

Play, as we shall see, lends itself, despite these less than encouraging premises, to investigation from a sociological perspective. Indeed, it is surprising that there is no established tradition on the subject. Apart from the specialized literature focusing on education, and apart from a few shining exceptions, especially in the Anglo-Saxon area, which have been able to optimize the theoretical and practical resources provided by the mathematical sciences, it seems that sociology has abdicated in favor of psychology and anthropology, at least as far as the observation and study of play practices are concerned. Today, however, there is the impression of an imminent turn away from this trend. While it is true that there are historical occasions when certain phenomena suddenly become legible from hitherto neglected perspectives, probably this period of crisis, bewilderment, deprivation of future, and general impoverishment is congenial as no other for questioning not only the elementary structures of individual behavior, not only the cultural traits of an ethnic group, but also the human condition itself as a relational dimension, to which sociology has always given the name of social bonding.

Another consideration must be made, to distinguish the sociological perspective that we intend to follow: when we talk about "play" or "game," we do not intend to take the point of view of the well-known *game theory*, although it is essential for understanding and formalizing many human behaviors, especially cooperation, decision-making, and competition (Webb, 2007). Indeed, the social sciences do not investigate the game as a field of deciphering a behavioral or combinatorial code: rather, they have the task of considering themselves part of the game, which *game theory* does not do, or does too cautiously. Sociology is continuous questioning, rather than the search for solutions. From this point of view, our sociological research considers the intersubjective, interdividual nature, Girard would say, of social bonding, a continuous game that does not necessarily respond to the logics of predictable and calculating action.

Now, if this is the case, that is, if social bonding needs to be talked about precisely when it is tragically lacking, the bet we propose is to highlight play as an essential, generative moment of the bond itself. By playing, one not only learns to survive the adversities of life, as in the playful exercises to which predatory mammals devote themselves with great solace, but one begins to weave a relationship; one learns, in short, to be together. Through play one ushers in horizons of common and shared meaning that would otherwise be completely idiosyncratic. In play, we learn an exquisitely human dimension, equidistant as much from the instinctual trials of the animal world as from the automatism of mechanical reactions: a dimension that is made up of risk and uncertainty, trust and betrayal, and dissimulation and passion. All in an intersection of glances, in an instant that—however ephemeral—already contains the universe of social possibilities.

There is no question here of defending a "Ludocentric" position, any "centralism" being foreign to a genuinely and serenely scientific approach. Just as we do not wish to eliminate gaming from the catalog of scientific investments and research, similarly we do not think that we can reduce all social action to gaming. What we are proposing here is first of all an acknowledgement referring to a specificity, which we have called "sociological game." Sociological play differs from others not so much because it takes place in different ways and at different times, but because it arises from a consideration that is precisely sociological in nature, namely that human behavior takes place on the surface of an encounter, not as an expression of a hidden interiority. The real "secret" of communication is not the removed or masked intention: it is its very event. The complexity of the surface belies the ideology of depth.

If for twenty or thirty years we have been forced to record, from the titles of now classic essays, a state of almost chronic malaise (if not even made acute by further aggravations of public illness); if we can do nothing but note the loss of values, the destruction of certainties, and the end of principles; if we find ourselves helpless before the spread of an arrogant hedonism that devastates traditional relationships and pulverizes local cultures; if everything that answers to the name of globalization hides behind it an ominous threat of misdirection, impoverishment, and leveling; and if these extreme scenarios characterize our contemporary experience, we nevertheless have the opportunity to approach a glimmer of genuine freedom that dwells in the most basic, perhaps even the most trivial, dimension of human relationship. From childhood experience to adult dynamics, play accompanies the adventure of the social. When the grenades of propaganda are extinguished, when ideologies and fanaticism are gone, there remain, as Wallace Stevens puts it, the "finally human": that is, when anthropocentric arrogance and conceit give way to humble human interdependence, "each person touches us / with what he is, as he is." These lines by Wallace Stevens pair with a charming image by

Philippe Jacottet: "A childlike joy infected the whole village: the old men threw snowballs." There is, in short, a note of extreme lightness against the background of the annihilation of late modernity. A lightness that is the ever new beginning of possible relationships, of possible futures.

However, it is a lightness that should not necessarily be understood as an indication of hope, because it does not necessarily prelude peace, concord, or renewal. Play should in no way be understood as a panacea, as a resolution or salvation in a "hideous universe" (as the "privateer" Pasolini would say); if it were, it would be reduced to a mystification all the more sordid, the more responsible, for contaminating the simpler nature of human beings. Pointing to play as a solution to social problems would be tantamount to advising a couple in crisis to look tenderly into each other's eyes—it may work, for goodness sake, but it does not seem to be the best of strategies! Play is not a solution, but a condition. Considering play from a sociological point of view basically means rethinking our interaction rituals starting precisely from the initial game that generated and guarded them to their current situation of routine or "everydayness," whatever this sort of magic formula means.

This book intends to deepen the affinity between play and social bonding; indeed, it intends to show their original coincidence, in an instance that the first chapter attempts to reconstruct through a genealogy that is both prudent and risky at the same time: that is to say, aware that identifying the foundations is a gamble allowed only outside the disciplinary field that one habitually frequents (and in fact we will discomfort psychoanalysis, ethology, anthropology, philosophy, poetry, etc.). Starting from the "grammar" of play outlined thanks to this genealogical effort, we will try to retrace the "syntax," that is, the structural procedure that underlies playful practice in its being social action: here we will make use of Darwin and the life sciences that investigate the expression of emotions; we will not, however, arrive at a biological reductionism, but on the contrary we will try to show how since Darwin biology has been making use of assumptions learned from the social sciences to give a foundation and a coherent perspective to its arguments. In our case, reference to Darwin and his sources (Adam Smith) will provide an opportunity to show the sociological core of the game, within social interaction based on sympathy.

The central chapters of this book are as many games, the writing and experimentation of which constitute the ultimate sense of the cultural operation to which the authors intended to devote their energies. These are interactive group games-workshops that can be simply read, or they can be experimented with or modified in the process. What is clear, and what probably constitutes a small lesson that the authors of these lines can take it upon themselves to impart, having learned it themselves on several occasions, is that the game cannot be taught except by doing it. Like the fundamental experiences of spiritual life, like love, like poetry, play cannot be prescribed, nor can it be reduced to mere theory. Play is played; otherwise it is something else. We have tried to reason about play, but more importantly we have tried to play and to make play. The last chapter is an attempt to structure our experience within an interpretive framework that can be useful at least to give an idea of the possible implications contained in the games themselves, especially considering that the writers have had the opportunity to experiment and try different versions of the games proposed here.

In any case, the game is such precisely because it is unique and unrepeatable; there are no copyrights in the playful experiences, just as the social bond is neither mine nor yours. The beauty of play is that we play together. The wish we make for ourselves and allow ourselves to share with readers is that this contribution of ours will serve to spread not only a more conscious culture of play but also a freer and more serene desire to play.

CHAPTER 1

Rules Are Needed to Play

PLAYING DOES NOT MEAN ESCAPING REALITY; THE REALITY OF PLAY IS not pure escapism. Often, in common language, especially in the language of educational institutions, we use the word "play" to contrast it with the word "seriousness," as if to say, "*Perder tempo a chi più sa più spiace*" ("The more you lose your time, the more you regret it," *Purgatorio*, canto 3, line 78). We thus delude ourselves that we control time, that we give it a discipline, an adult and incontrovertible meaning: what produces and conforms to criteria of utility and accounting is fine, and the rest is luxury or waste. But play is part of life; indeed, as we shall try to show, it is its very core and, at the same time, a harbinger with evolutionary ramifications. To waste time playing is to gain time—time that is trial and error—and share experiences. All of this makes us special creatures, certainly, unmatched among living things. And yet the nature of that which lives is such, perhaps, precisely because it plays, because there is play at the bottom of the resounding seriousness that governs all that is born, and spends time and dies in fragile and unrepeatable hours.

1.1. The Seagull's Move

There are constants in animal behavior that affect humans; ethologists rubricize these as ambivalence. They are, in particular, relationships between conspecifics. A classic example is the common gull, whose black feathers on its head are indicative of aggressive behavior. Such a characteristic makes the pairing difficult: the male that wants to approach the female is forced—if he does not want to receive painful defensive pecks—to move his head away, mimicking meek behavior such as begging for food, as the young do. It is a gesture that throughout the animal world serves to inhibit aggression (Eibl-Eibesfeldt, 1989). This characteristic also recurs in humans, most prominently in early infancy, when the infant learns to distinguish its mother from other people. The phenomenon of attachment manifests itself ambivalently, with gestures of contact-seeking alternating, within seconds even, with opposite behavioral modules of avoidance (e.g., of the gaze). The ambivalence of the social relationship has the same basis in the seagull as in the child: on the one hand, my neighbor is a threat, a rival in the search for food and love, a potential murderer, "my hell," as Sartre put it; on the other hand, my neighbor is a support, the object of my desires, my life companion, "my paradise" (Dupuy, 2016).

The relationship with the conspecific is, of course, the most difficult problem for a living being to solve, perhaps not the most exhausting, but undoubtedly the most complex. One only has to spend a handful of seconds in an elevator with perfect strangers to measure the ease with which one is able to contemplate the tips of one's shoes or the corners of the ceiling, the hands of one's watch, or the seam of a shoulder on a stranger's (or one's own) jacket to avoid eye contact with anyone (Goffman, 1963). Those who do not belong to the (narrow—for evolutionary reasons we cannot go into) circle of knowledge are avoided or even removed from perception (i.e., they are not noticed). With strangers, gradualness and willingness are required, as with the black feathers of the seagull. It is gradualness, together with the display of innocent signals (e.g., smiling, extending hands, and seeking eye contact) that determines an effective encounter; on these signals, human cultures have built over time a vast repertoire of rules and instructions of "good manners" for living together.

Each cultural group has its own good manners by which it measures, sanctions, and identifies its members. For example, in the seventeenth-century French court, it was customary to observe with exasperated attention the behaviors and gestures of others as part of a silent duel and larval struggle for prestige (i.e., to stay as close as possible to the ruler, or even just to remain in the court circle and not be marginalized). This entailed the development of meticulous bodily and emotional discipline, above all the control of aggressive and brutal impulses, such as outbursts of anger. Self-discipline, which regulated the relationship between members of the court, was concerned principally with the concealment of emotion. The categorical imperative was to "know the passions to dissimulate them." It is no coincidence that it was in these circles that the first modern treatises on human affections were born (Perrault, La Rochefoucauld, and so on). There arose in such contexts the treatment of the "how": how to manipulate others, to please them, not to offend them, and to direct or divert attention to oneself (Bourdieu, 1979; Elias, 1933/1983). All this should be reread today as a germane element of social ethnography and participant observation. Concealing the desire for belonging by submissive behavior—the desire to be part of the court entailed a barely concealed smug detachment from one's rivals—again finds parallels in the seductive game of the common gull, who, to obtain what he desires, is driven to conduct a "courtship," that is, literally a "courtly" behavior—a label that sanctions the goodness of his intentions and the harmlessness of his approach.

Without etiquette, without manners, one cannot practice animal behavior at all (as is sometimes said). The biological virtue of ambivalence is not a cultural addition to a biological substratum; to call someone a donkey because he or she acts inappropriately is, in itself, not only "impolite," but a mistake. Ethological research teaches that there is no animal behavior devoid of ambivalence, just as the social sciences attest that there is no interpersonal relationship that does not involve dissimulation. Goffman's (1963, 1967) research on strategic interaction and interaction rituals offers several examples of this. But it is ethnomethodology that shows how language itself is based on seagull play: as the infant learns to stammer the word "mother," he or she does so to please his or her parents, to rely on and receive reassurance, to correspond to a bond of trust, and also because the word is very easy to pronounce; but he or she does so first and foremost for apotropaic purposes. Indeed, the word points to the mother in the flesh, evoking her eventual return or averting her disappearance, under the eyes of the father. The language reproduces the ambivalence of desire that feeds on the interplay of an object's presence and absence.

Psychoanalysts have been studying this subject for a century or more. From the "bobbin play" onwards, we know that language is the rhythmic expression of an obsession, which is the ambivalence of life in general: being and non-being, presence and absence, *fort-da* (i.e., the bobbin play). The animal does not play the bobbin play, or rather it does but it does not reproduce its syllabic rhythm, as Freud's grandson did in the justly famous example described in *Beyond the Pleasure Principle* (Freud, 1920/1955). Language, a human and social cipher par excellence, enshrines the continuity of memory of the species, the group, the family, and the individual. To say "mother" is to recognize in the word the desired and evoked presence of "my" mother (which is why children spend some time struggling to understand that other children also have "their" mother; cultural relativism, evidently, is not innate). Learning to say "mother," therefore, means fixing in the vocal support system (the first and main extracorporeal one, the first technical "prosthesis") a memory datum; in short, it means remembering.

This gesture, this expiration of syllables, which reproduces the ambivalent behavior of the intraspecific relationship, marks both the distance between the animal and the human and the complex particularity of human relationships compared with those of other living species. Although the chimpanzee also establishes enduring family bonds, the social etiquette that binds its relationships is not exposed to language games, as is the case with humans. The baby chimpanzee attracts its mother's attention with various sounds and gestures, but the first months of the mother-child relationship are characterized by a silence that in our eyes is emblematic and abysmal when compared with the profusion of sweet words and pampering with which a human mother envelops the sound world of her baby as she teaches it to speak (Falk, 2009).

Thus, we move from an elementary biological trait—ambivalence—to a human trait, into which a proliferation of historical, cultural, ethnic, and geographical differences are inserted. This is clearly why a wolfhound employs far fewer tools to communicate with its conspecific than its master would with his. But what we want to highlight is not so much the human specificity of culture based on language but the fact that that same culture—that same symbolic repertoire derived from the use of the voice—is itself the outcome of a peculiar elaboration referring back to the original ambivalence. It is, in short, the same thing as the courtship dance of the common gull.

1.2. Disappearing Objects

"We live without feeling the country beneath our feet"; so begins a 1933 poem by Osip Mandelstam, one that proved personally fatal because it displeased Stalin—a man whom the poet refers to as "the Kremlin mountain man" and the "robber." Subsequently, Mandelstam was first sent to the Siberian gulag, then to the town of Voronezh, and finally to Vladivostok, where he died in 1938. Not feeling the ground under one's feet, in any case, has a value beyond Mandelstam's tragic life story (which, let it be said, honors the work and testimony of a very great poet). The point is that people, objects, and the world, regardless of political and historical contingencies, are ephemeral. The sun goes down, the mother goes to work, the father "evaporates," as Lacan would say, the girlfriend doesn't answer the phone, the friend is late, the employer "will let us know," money comes out of pockets like Thumbelina's crumbs, society liquefies, values disappear, walls collapse, people die, and so on. Again, people, objects, and the world are not permanent; the moment you become aware of them, they disappear. It is precisely this annoying "virtue" of theirs that makes them valuable symbols in social relations, in the pursuit of prestige and reputation; this is how language with its symbols reproduces the culture of a group, indicating to each person, with words and gestures, the objects of value, or at least those one believes are worth fighting for.

The anthropologist Ernesto de Martino spoke of the "loss of presence" as a fundamental emotion underlying ritual elaborations. No longer guaranteed a safe environment (or at least one that can be instinctually defined), human beings are forced to measure themselves day after day while knowing everything is transient: Hence the weight that memory and tradition have assumed over millennia of cultural evolution. Hence, too, the need to work on the fragility of objects, to resist the ephemeral, to migrate to a permanent (metahistorical) elsewhere in one's desire for eternity, or what De Martino

(1977/2002) called the "ethos of transcendence," lightly evading the anguish of a senseless world. All this constitutes the important elementary structure that underlies the human capacity for play.

The memory of gestures and words guarantees continuity, which is why children play so much and so vigorously. Games, as Michel de Montaigne (*Essais*, book 1, ch. 23) states, are not "just" games: it is necessary to know how to consider them as absolutely "serious" actions, where seriousness implies not so much an accounting or computational relationship with things, nor a particular cognitive investment (which constitutes, if anything, an added value, a surplus of efficacy, analyzed just as effectively by cognitivism), but above all a subjective involvement, directed at the need for the other and the playmate (real or imaginary) to remain or return—or at least to allow for the possibility of their evocation. The playmate, as with the seagull, constitutes a threat, a potential cause of defeat, but also the only opportunity to be able to play again.

Again, it is the bobbin play that shows, in its simplicity, the profound significance of the perception of the ephemeral: the child who is distressed by his or her mother's absences projects resentment and longing into the spool, coining a kind of "magic formula," fort-da, "away-qua" while contemplating the rhythm of the disappearance and reappearance of the object. Similarly, we may surmise, Paleolithic primitives evoked the return of the sun through apotropaic modulations, just as the chorus of Jerusalem maidens, in the seventh chapter of the *Song of Songs*, pleads "come back Shulamite"; the same is most likely true of the "peekaboo," which constitutes one of the earliest forms of ritual interaction between infant and mother (Stern, 1987, p. 117), and which also has interesting ethnological affinities with playful behaviors in higher primates (Falk, 2009, p. 30).

Hiding and reappearing, chasing each other, catching each other, and wrestling are all games in which one takes pleasure in enacting the ephemeral: one's permanence that escapes the sight, the grasp, the resistance of the "wolf." The wolf is a constant in many childhood games, as it is in fairy-tale imagery. Playing "wolf," that is, chasing one another, is to sustain the cultural constant of prey and predator as an archetype of life exposed to a disturbing and uncanny fragility (Eisler, 1951). Every game, after all, is a mode of anxiety management, a way of containing the disturbance of feeling that the ground is missing under one's feet. One fills the emptiness of the loss of presence through the vicissitudes of fairy tales or games, ritual or simple pastimes, which is by no means simple to do; indeed, it often requires much more energy than a professional activity (Bruner, 1990; Elias, 1978/2009).

Whether it is an unconscious way of processing "grief," as in the case of the Freudian little one, or a strategy for not dwelling on the unthinkable background of one's experiences, play has always drawn human beings to their own condition: creatures who care for and fear their own elusive consistency; care for and fear the comings and goings of others, themselves, and things. What unmistakably distinguishes—it seems—human play from that of animals is precisely this projection (which inevitably translates into linguistic formulas and metaphors, as we shall see) of care and fear onto an objective social background. The rules of play, with their ritual undercurrents, are the screen on which participants recognize their condition and share it, learning to live with it and domesticating the powerful emotional tensions that accompany the awareness that people, objects, and the world end.

1.3. A Society That Plays

The question opened up by the constitutive ambivalence of the relationship with the conspecific, exemplified by the seagull game, is thus taken up and embodied in the equally ambivalent structure of the human-social relationship, which in turn is exemplified by the bobbin play. In both cases, the behavioral background is represented by deep and unresolvable insecurity with respect to one's survival in the relationship or group. Childhood attachment processes attest precisely to how delicate the construction of the self is and how exposed it is to trauma; that is, they reveal how hard we struggle to accept the distance from a safe haven or the excessive closure of borders. As has been amply demonstrated, what matters in parental care is not so much the nurturing as the relational aspect (Bowlby, 1969; Eibl-Eibesfeldt, 1989). An overly busy or emotionally cold mother is likely to do irreversible damage to her child, even if she nurtures him or her regularly; likewise, a mother (or father—it is the same of course, or nearly) who systematically prevents her child from exploring the surrounding environment will have an equally detrimental effect on the child's cognitive and social development. It goes without saying that, in all of this, play plays a crucial role.

Not only does simulation play enable many animal species to appease the wrath of their mate or opponent, not only does spool play enable the involuntary infant witnessing the death drive to build a resistance system that can protect him or her from the anguish of abandonment—play is the dominant subject, the main argument, and the decisive proving ground for taking on the original and irreducible ambivalence that underlies communal living, the establishment of systems of coexistence, of interwoven relationships of kinship, of proximity, of solidarity, and of contractual and organizational negotiation.

The psychoanalyst Donald Winnicott (1971) observed how play provided not only a privileged field of inquiry for the observation of younger patients in therapy—as is well known child analysis was a bone of contention in the internal debates within psychoanalytic societies—but also a place of creative development, a kind of cosmology in which an as yet not fully affirmed identity had the opportunity to experiment with transitions and strategies of defense and attack or just teeter between them.

Winnicott's reflections and analyses contain something that is of primary importance for a sociological consideration of play: that it is not (especially in early childhood) a matter of individual choice, nor is it a task that the individual takes on to achieve a particular purpose; on the contrary, it takes place in what Winnicott (1971) calls "an intermediate area between the finger and the teddy bear ... between the child's inability and growing ability to recognize and accept reality" (p. 24).

Play, therefore, has a third social dimension, after that of the seagull (simulation by an approach to the conspecific) and the bobbin (processing distress): even when one is alone, one is always playing with (or against) someone. The social dimension does not mean simply that there must be two or more players, as is written in the instructions for box games; it means that individuality—as with any other datum of reality that one claims or assumes as objective—emerges from an intermediate space-time, "the fontal place of manifestation of all reality" (D'Alessandro, 1991, p. 301). On closer inspection, this third dimension was already inscribed in the first (the seagull dance is evidently a social constraint) and, implicitly, in the second. Indeed, Freud, when describing the dynamics of the bobbin play, first noted how the child intended to process the anguish of distance from the mother, yet shortly thereafter—and for psychoanalysis, this was a "quantum" leap, as it came to be described—stated that the little one used to replicate with some insistence (i.e., with a compulsion to repeat) only the first phase of the game, throwing away (fort) a whole series of objects that came within his reach, as indeed most children do as they become familiar with prehension and oculomotor coordination. Now, if the first description of the bobbin play was appropriate to the pleasure principle (*Lustprinzip*), insofar as the staging of the "return" of the object could be read as compensation in the economy of desire, the second ushered in the famous theme of the death drive (*Todestrieb*), that is— for our purposes—the absolute, disturbing futility of the game. It is "beyond good and evil," to quote a Nietzschean title (which is unsurprisingly taken up by Freud in his essay).

This further ambivalence is, once again, illuminating. Play, in its primary dimension, is a social experience insofar as it consigns the individual to society, regardless of strategies of survival (as in the case of the seagull) or compensation (as in the case of the "complete" bobbin play). If it is true, as Bateson's famous saying goes, that the "relationship comes first," then it also precedes the entire system of values and utility. Play, Emile Benveniste (1947) argues, is an activity that "does not involve a useful modification of the real" (p. 161). In this sense, play is "preconditioning." The play event coincides with the area where one acquires and consolidates what is perhaps the core of the social cell, which takes the form of a paradox: that of being alone in the presence of someone (Winnicott, 1958), or even being with someone in the presence of no one (Cooley, 1902; Mead, 1934).

1.4. The Grammar of Play

We have thus isolated three constitutive dimensions of play: approach, compensation, and social relationships. Each presupposes the presence of the others, acting as part of a cycle. The game of approach is a search for compensation because it addresses the continuity of the other; the game of compensation, in turn, is the inauguration of a social relationship insofar as it is never played in a neutral field but within pre-established codes and regulations. These codes, moreover, are the result of negotiations more or less painstakingly evolved over the course of countless attempted "approaches."

At this point, we can identify a kind of "grammar of the game," that is, a structure containing the essential conditions for the possibility of human play. It is not a matter of yielding to the classificatory allure of a normative systematics, as if the "grammar" in question establishes once and for all indissoluble and incontrovertible rules and constraints. By "grammar," we mean the process by which play constructs and conveys the social relations that take place in and with it. In the knowledge that grammar always involves a certain degree of abstraction from practices—reasoning that the worst way to learn a foreign language is to memorize the mechanics of grammatical rules—we do not intend to establish a theoretical framework that forces social actions into more or less contrived adaptations. Rather, it is a general orientation that summarizes what we believe to be the functional invariants of play, in the manner of a Piagetian (1975) analysis of cognitive development.

The first of these invariants is repetition. In no other cultural sphere does the *repetita iuvant* principle apply as it does in play. The intimate nature of the pleasure we gain from playing probably also rests in the fact that we identify in play an available, permanent place; the more permanence is guaranteed, the more repetition confirms the constitutive dimension of compensation. If the world around us constantly threatens to fade away, play, with its repetitiveness, at least provides a foothold, or—as Fink (1957) might put it—an oasis of joy.

However, as an individual reading Freud, or even an attentive observer of childhood games, might come to understand, the "enjoyment" that those who play derive from repetition is but a mask. It is neither the pleasure principle nor the satisfaction that is to be gained from an effective algorithm; it has a dark undertone similar to the agitation that seizes us when we have to hold something fragile, something that is in danger of falling apart at any moment. The obsession of the lover seeking his or her beloved, the stubbornness with which four- or five-year-old children want to hear the same story over and over again—and woe betide the narrator if a single adjective or adverb is missing—and the liturgy of the board game are all masks of repetition, a palliative invariant that, if not balanced by a deviation or an evolutionary process, risks degenerating into obsessive neurosis and a compulsion to repeat (an expression of the death drive) (Deleuze, 1983). In other words, compensation is inconsolable, inexhaustible, and continuously self-reproducing. It is from here that the need for something new arises, which distracts from the continuum established by the undaunted repetition of the same game.

The second invariant is strategy, and it is engaged when repetition exhausts its compensatory function. The emotional outcome of repetition, when it does not lapse into compulsion, is boredom. When one observes children, even when they are at a very tender age, one can see how they perform tasks in a way that satisfies their own functional pleasure. But when they achieve the desired goal (e.g., stacking wooden bricks), they feel the need to reconfigure the pattern and destroy their laboriously assembled turrets. The point is that this reconfiguration, at a given level of complexification, no longer suffices to recreate the premise of play that one realizes one is capable of doing better and more frequently. One wishes to experiment; one dares to step into the void. Of course, always "for play," but play in this case is indispensable for the development of manual and social skills and—in a co-evolutionary circularity—the cerebral cortex (Ceruti, 1986; Morin, 1973; Sennett, 2008).

The term "strategy" (*strategos*) has its origins in Greek and corresponds to the art of conducting battle, since *stratos* is not only the "plateau" but also the "field," and the suffix **egos* comes from *ago*, meaning "I lead." To be a strategist in the game means to assume a leadership role or, from an ontogenetic perspective, to begin to assert one's individuality, one's style, one's character—one's self. There are infinite possibilities for repetition, but strategy is irreducibly singular, unrepeatable; it enables one to create new horizons, break free of constraints, and move toward new possibilities.

The same dynamic between repetition and strategy occurs in learning processes: playing a Bach variation, delivering a knockout blow, performing an *o-soto-gari*, executing a *fouetté en tournant*, performing a logarithmic function, translating an ode by Horace are all more or less complex operations that require long and repetitive practice. *Repetita iuvant*, as the Latin proverb says. Repetition binds the body and mind to exercises or training routines that are seemingly "unnatural." Once the process is completed, the body assumes the role of strategist and thereafter chooses its own style, its own singular mode of performance. Otherwise, there would be no pianists, soccer players, karatekas, dancers, mathematicians, or poets, simply performers of automatic procedures.

Strategy is thus the evolutionary leap that enables the individual to express himself or herself, at the price of a sometimes exhausting series of practices. After all, the asceticism of which mysticism in any age speaks is nothing but askesis; training or exercise (including spiritual exercise, of course) is nothing else but that, and work, in all its declinations, is first and foremost labor, or toil. The child prodigy is not the one who learns without effort, but the one who, in drudgery (in some cases inhumanly imposed by reckless parents), can quickly identify strategies for self-affirmation.

The child prodigy serves as an illustration of the third functional invariant of play, namely sociability (Simmel, 1901/1967). As Elias (1991) surmised in the case of Mozart, genius does not dwell in the secret and intangible intimacy of a single individual, no matter how astounding and out of the ordinary his or her abilities are; it is the outcome of a complex interweaving that we might describe as "the return of strategy to the bed of the social." If strategy is the emergence and affirmation of individuality, one must, if one is to find confirmation and fulfilment, "get back in the game." The game creates companionship: this, in its extreme synthesis, is the goal of its determinations and invariants. The purpose of the game is not to win, participate, train one for public life, or represent the Malthusian struggle for survival. The game, as we shall try to show, has no purpose other than to create cohesion, to ensure there are companions to play with, to repeat the game to the point of boredom, to invent new strategies (and thus emerge as a leader, a genius, a trickster, and so on), then to play again.

The structure thus set forth, with its dimensions or levels (approach, compensation, and relation), and its functional invariants (repetition, strategy, and sociability), testifies to the irreducibility of play, that is, to the fact that one cannot rubricize this "type" of social action within a "typology," or—much the same—establish a science of play. Play has no purpose other than in itself, so it is important to meet it on its own terms, which means "living on the edge of the abyss," as Bataille (1947) describes it. One must, therefore, expect absurd things to happen.

This is not a comfortable position to be in, as one might well imagine. Nor is it much challenged by the human sciences, which—largely using psychodynamic notions centered on the individual—tend to enucleate concepts and ideas in a reductionist schematism because they are still tied to the assumption of the "inside" and the "outside" and of the individual and society as if they were discrete entities or parallel worlds (Elias, 1969/2009). We are proposing a sociological perspective, one that is able not so much to explain or translate the game but express and narrate it. It has its dark as well as exhilarating sides and necessitates an investigation of the social matrix of one of the most powerful and, at the same time, elusive components of human and social experience: emotions and their expression.

CHAPTER 2

Envy and Paranoia

The Traps of Play

As we saw in the previous chapter, what is pertinent to the social sciences with respect to play is the emotional and relational dimension: it is from this dimension that we need to move. If with the genealogy of play we have come to construct a "grammar," it is now a matter of defining a "syntax" through the evolution of human social skills in their elementary structure, that is, emotions, their expression and the social drifts that such expression implies. What emerges thanks to play is, in fact, a fundamental and often overlooked element: social bonding is not an inert datum, an absolute principle, in the etymological sense of the term; in other words, for human beings the practice of living together, although it has natural connotations (for Aristotle, we are social by nature), it simultaneously possesses no pre-established elements. Play highlights the risks we both take on a daily basis and cause to be taken in sharing our lives with others. Play therefore means putting one's own life or the life of another on the line. Clearly, in the course of our investigation, the theme that has so far remained under the radar will increasingly emerge: that of violence.

2.1. The Move of the Party Pooper

The question is: Where does the game come from? What is its origin? Its functions are quite clear; the sciences have described them, and nature provides the appropriate examples. Despite this, there remains an elusive element. Let's try a few examples. Everyone will have happened to see a group of children playing; at some point, a quarrel breaks out among them: one child has decided to make his own rules or does not want to follow the rules. "It doesn't count!" says one. "You can't play anymore!" says another, and so on. The turmoil lasts a few minutes, then the group reassembles: the rebellious little one has either been ousted or has bowed to the will of the others. The general mood, however, has changed: there is more anger in the faces of the players. In a short time, it is as if they have grown up: they are like the young man gathering hallucinated memories of Coleridge's ancient mariner, sadder and wiser. Sadder, because the magic is broken. They were playing well; they were having fun, then "that one" came along and ruined everything. But also wiser, because now they know how to move when something like this happens. They have accumulated experience; they know something more about life, how it can hold surprises, how it can disappoint. There, the irruption of the unexpected into the game is part of the game, of course, but when the unexpected is a subject whose obvious purpose is to upset the balance, to hinder the game, the mystery becomes profound. It is no longer a strategy for winning, functional to the maintenance and indeed the success of the playful experience; it is a self-destructive element that often reveals what is going on and, for that very reason, is highly disruptive.

In the world of adolescents, this disruption of the levels of communication and interaction takes on a peculiar aspect: teens are the first to violate the rules of the game in order to test its resilience. The tension that is created is typical of this age, and it has a very important evolutionary function: thanks to the experimentation of young people, in fact, many social and cultural barriers have been overcome in the course of the evolution of our species (Morin, 1973). From the sociological point of view, the break with established habits and the crisis of traditional values are also very often salutary for the general balance of groups, whereby adolescents play an emancipatory function with respect to stiffened dynamics that are not suited to face the challenges of a changing environment.

However, while adolescents are capable of representing the vanguard of change, the courage to find new ways ("I have to go away," as the boy in Cat Stevens's "Father & Son" repeats), this same revolutionary force can activate a very high self-destructive potential. Indeed, adolescents, when they find no other possible trajectories on which to direct their energies, their anger, their desires, attack the body. Eating disorders, drug use, risky behavior, and self-injury are all examples of the irruption of an unexpectedness that has no creative or productive function but is rather aimed at destroying or at least radically questioning the affective ties and social rules that have so far prevailed and dominated. We thus witness the intervention of a player whose purpose is neither to win nor to have fun, but to destroy the possibility of play.

This disturbance and disturbing presence acts in social dynamics, influences them and—this is our hypothesis—makes them apparent. Through play, as we shall see, the mostly unnoticed plots of this process can be shown, whereby the crisis of ties brings ties themselves to the fore. Thus, play is not only a metaphor for society but also a research and action tool with which to observe relationships in action and care for them. Therefore, it is appropriate to delve into this revealing figure of a structural crisis, whose features and meaning are so obvious as to even trouble myth.

In many traditional cultures and stories, there is a bizarre character, somewhere between divinity and buffoonery, who performs abstruse, morally reprehensible actions, but almost always with a ridiculous overtone. According to some scholars, these are decayed forms of ancient deities (Radin, Jung & Kérényi, 1954/1972), the outcome of a spiritual development aimed at belittling the seriousness of a character, highlighting his limitations and labors. However, the historical-religious aspect is not what is most interesting to us. What is important, instead, is the recurrence of certain patterns that present themselves almost as invariants and that, in many ways, constitute a kind of pattern for the interactive dynamics that arise every day in gaming situations, offices, schools, and real or virtual squares. It concerns the myth of the trickster.

The character who breaks the mold, plays tricks, cheats, and ambushes is present in many literary and religious traditions. Sometimes it takes on the features of a god, like Hermes, for example; other times it is a thematic remnant that remains as a character figure, of which perhaps a paradigm could be Jacob mocking Esau, or Odysseus cheating Polyphemus. In the contemporary world, the rascal may have the swaggering, easy-going features of George Clooney in *Ocean's Eleven* or the chilling grin of Joaquin Phoenix in *Joker*. In any case, narratives that contain scenes of cheating, swindling, and deception also often convey a sense of vertigo that suspends moral judgment. The trickster is often beyond good and evil: he is too clever or too foolish to be judged by a shared and acceptable standard. This condition brings the trickster closer to the sphere of the sacred, because it keeps him separate from the normal world in which social rules, etiquette, customs, etc., apply. Let us note that the same condition of "shooting," of cheating, is also found in the game, as anyone who has tried a few times to bluff during a game of poker, or to dribble a fullback by entering the penalty area, knows well.

This close affinity between the dimensions of the game and that of society and culture has already been noted and described by Johan Huizinga (1938/2002), who was among the first to note how that of the game was not simply a metaphor, but something more like a microcosm. Inside the game, in fact, the same events take place, in a small way, as in the great scenes of history. The event that takes place in the game is small only in size; emotionally, it is virtually identical to those running through the world at large. The emotions are the same. This is the magic of the game: the anger, frustration, joy, triumph, gloom, fear, shame, etc., that a child feels when they play are the same as those felt by the soldier when they fight, the surgeon when they operate, the sports player when they jump or run or scrap, the model when they parade, the manager when they buy a package of stock, etc. The object of reference is obviously different, but the emotional dimension, at its generative core, is the same. The fiction of the game is *fictio*, that is, literally "fabrication," the construction of the material with which one is confronted; the imagined challenge anticipates the real one but is no less exciting. A penalty kick or a combination at the console, but also an interrogation or an exam, produce the same adrenaline charge as the tests that the adult is called upon to face and that they alone consider to be more serious and more important.

Now, the functional explanation of play, as we have seen, meets a need that is itself functional: to declare that play serves something, whatever it is, to establish that it is a function of something. In this key, it is assumed that play is a determinate practice, which somehow precedes or supports other more complex practices of a productive or destructive kind, according to a binary scheme of the type: A prepares B. The same pattern has been applied to traditional narrative and myth for centuries. Thus myth is regarded as a naive or crude explanation, not yet refined by logical-formal thinking (Piaget) or scientific rationality (Frazer). Myth, therefore, would be a survival of the way primitive men explained natural phenomena, such as life, misfortunes, love, death, etc. The universal questions posed by myth prepare, according to the functional pattern, the maturity of rational answers; A prepares B.

Speaking of myth, and in particular the figure of the trickster, the party pooper whose function (or rather dysfunction) we are investigating, a highly revealing example comes from the Norse tradition, particularly the events related to the god Loki. The ancient stories and Icelandic epics are collected in a series of texts to which tradition has given the title *Edda*, which some believe recalls the archaic Norse term for "grandmother" or "ancestress." In any case, there are two collections bearing this title: one, so-called poetic, older, bringing together widely varied narratives dating from an unspecified time between the fifth and tenth centuries; the other, prose, more recent, compiled by a thirteenth-century scholar, Snorri Sturluson. These are important details, because, when studying ancient stories involving mythological and religious motifs and themes, one should always be mindful of the sources from which one draws. All the more so in our case, as will soon become evident. Let us first take a look at the story that interests us most closely: the scene is the typical (or perhaps archetypal?) one of a banquet among gods, looking very much like a gathering of rowdy and gigantic Vikings, and it is portrayed in a tenth-century carol entitled "Lokasenna," "the insults of Loki."

Aegir invites the gods to toast themselves with the new beer he has brewed; the diners greatly appreciate the hospitality and enjoy the pageantry of the gold-adorned hall and the dexterity of the servants, who are showered with praise. Loki, however, becomes jealous of a servant and suddenly kills him. The gods banish Loki from the banquet, but he returns to it, appealing to the hospitality sacred to Odin: *Remember, Odin, that we two at the beginning of time / mixed our blood; / beer you would never have consumed, you said / if along with me you had not taken it* (9). Thanks to the mediation of the first among the gods, Loki is readmitted to the banquet, but his tongue has no restraint and he proceeds to insult anyone who comes within his reach: he excludes Bragi from the toast and calls him a coward, just as he calls his wife, Idhunn, a whore. The same treatment he gives to Gefjon (*Now I will tell /*

how at the pleasure of love he seduced you / that blond youth, who offered you a jewel / and you with your thighs clasped him [20].) and to Frigg and Freyja. He even calls Odin an invert (24), goes wild with Njordhr (*Hymir's daughters held you as a chamber pot / and pissed in your mouth* [34]), and with many others, until Thorr arrives and forces him to flee by threatening him with his mighty hammer. In leaving, Loki curses the host's house (*on every one of your possessions that is in here / may flame play / and burn you on your back!*). The prose conclusion is in many ways reminiscent of the ancient Greek myth of Prometheus: the Aesir (the Norse gods) chase Loki and bind him by placing a poisonous snake over his face, causing poison to drip on the insolent god. Sygin, Loki's wife, sits beside him holding a small bowl under the drops of poison; as the bowl fills, she goes to empty the poison. Meanwhile, however, the poison continues to drip on Loki. And these shudder so violently that the whole earth is shaken: this phenomenon is now called an earthquake.

The closing of the song of Loki's insults is an early example of a functionalist reading of the myth: the torment of Loki (A) prepares for the explanation of the phenomenon of earthquakes (B). But what is of interest for our purposes is the bizarre figure of this god who ruins the festival of the Aesir, who insults anyone heavily and without restraint. The structure of the story is that of an individual pitted against a group. Were it not for the initial murder and the insults that Loki continues to utter, one could speak of a lynching against the god: everyone attacks him, everyone detests him, everyone contributes, in the end, to his torment. The same pattern is found in an apparently very different version of Loki's exploits.

Also in Snorri's *Edda*, in the forty-ninth chapter of *Gylfaginning*, we see the "all against one," but here the same pattern seems to multiply across many levels. It is worth reporting the passage in full:

> This story begins when Baldr, the good man, dreamed great dreams that were a harbinger of danger to his life. When he told the Aesir [i.e., gods of the Norse religion] about those dreams, they met in council and it was decided to demand for Baldr a guarantee from all kinds of harm. And Frigg obtained these oaths that everything would spare Baldr: fire and water, iron and every kind of metal, stones, earth, trees, diseases, animals, birds, poison, snakes. And this done and defined it was a pastime for Baldr and the Aesir that he stood upright in the thing [the assembly] and all others

aimed at him, some from afar, some from nearby striking him, some by throwing stones, but whatever was done nothing harmed him, and to all of them this seemed great advantage.

So here we have a deity, Baldr, called "the good one," who fears for his safety and has some kind of panacea prescribed to make him invulnerable to any means of offense. At that point, all the gods enjoy striking him, under the pretext that they cannot harm him. This is to all intents and purposes the staging of a lynching: all against one. But it does not end there; again, there is an assembly having fun, and Loki comes along to spoil the game.

> But when Loki, son of Laufey, saw this, he was sorry that nothing would harm Baldr. He went to Frigg and Frnsalir and took the form of a woman. Then Frigg asked the woman if she knew what the Aesir do in the *thing*. And the one related that they all pulled on Baldr and that he had no harm from it. Then Frigg said, "Neither weapon nor wood can harm Baldr—I have been sworn by all things." The woman then asked, "Have all things sworn to spare Baldr?" And Frigg replies, "There grows a little plant to the west of the Valhöll that has the name mistletoe; it seemed to me too young to demand the oath." Immediately thereafter the woman departed.

Again there are interesting mythological parallels with the theme of invulnerability. In many cases, this supernatural power includes an exception: Achilles's invulnerability does not cover his heel, and Siegfried's does not protect a spot on his back. In Baldr's story, however, the exception is not a body part removed from the magical bath (the Styx for Achilles, the dragon's blood for Siegfried), but a creature, the mistletoe, that was deemed "too young" to adhere to the oath of harmlessness. Once again the "all against one" scheme (here in the form: all but one). Let's see what Loki comes up with.

> Loki took the mistletoe seedling, tore it up, and returned to the council. There Hödhr stood alone outside the circle of the others, for he was blind. Then Loki spoke to him, "How is it that you do not also pull on Baldr?" He answered, "Because I do not see where Baldr is and then because I am without weapons." Then Loki said, "Do as the others do, give honor to

Baldr, I will show you where he is. Hit him with this stick." Hödhr took the mistletoe and hurled it at Baldr according to Loki's indication; the blow pierced him and knocked him to the ground dead. And this was the greatest misfortune that occurred among the gods and among men.

Again an "all but one": Hödhr is blind and cannot play "all against one" and stands aside. Loki intervenes and breaks the balance; he drives Hödhr's arm and causes Baldr's death. At the end of the tale, in the fiftieth chapter, we see the vengeance of the gods, almost identical to that narrated in the *carme* quoted previously. The Aesir seize Loki and bind him over three stones:

> Then Skadhi took a poisonous snake and secured it over him so that the poison dripped from the snake down onto his face. But Sigyn, his wife, stands by him and holds a basin under the drops of poison, and when it is full she goes and empties it. And meanwhile the poison drips on his face, and he shakes so violently that the whole earth trembles. This is what you call an earthquake.

The functional explanation that Snorri posits to the tale of Loki's misdeeds indicates the close thematic kinship between the tale of the banquet and the tale of Baldr's death: both end up providing an explanation for a natural event, or rather, both explain the formation of the tale itself (A) as a preparation for what we, the descendants of the first storytellers, call a natural event (B). Earthquakes are indeed very frightening phenomena: they suddenly burst in, devastate, and ruin everything that has been carefully prepared by man to last. A primitive mind might well have imagined that underlying these unpredictable irruptions of natural forces was the writhing of a chained god, the same god who, among his peers, behaves in turn like an earthquake. It seems that for several centuries this analogy worked very well.

2.2. The Three Stages of Violence

The explanation of the myth, like that of the game, in terms of the "A prepares B" scheme is highly effective. However, it shows at least two weaknesses, prompting some doubt about its real validity. First, in the two tales of Loki's turmoil—the insults at the Aesir's banquet in the poetic *Edda* and the murder of Baldr in the prose *Edda*—the explanation of the tale sounds like posturing, like a didactic addition: it plays no narrative role, somewhat like the moralistic proverbs that close Phaedrus's fables. The Loki myths do not begin by asking for an account of earthquakes, yet they both end by explaining why the earth suddenly shakes. An explanation that sounds like an *excusatio non petita* (unsolicited apology).

The second weakness of the functional explanation is that it works too well; in its linearity, built on the analogy between Loki's writhing and the earth's crust shuddering, it erases with extreme simplicity all the previous scenes. It makes no further mention of the poor slain servant; nor of the very heavy insults thrown in handfuls; nor is there any more mention of Baldr, Hödhr, mistletoe, etc. Loki's torment becomes a didactic device for dealing with the unpredictable fury of nature. The explanation does not, in fact, explain anything at all about what happened before; instead, it performs a completely different function, which is typical of myth: it renders the questions from which it had started no longer questionable, superimposing other questions on top of them (Blumenberg, 1979).

The initial questions—we do not call them original, so as not to expire in an auroral apotheosis that is always cloying—are the ones that are usually the simplest. It often happens, however, as in the case of the Loki myth, that these questions are buried by a very powerful common sense, which we call "religious empiricism." Empiricism, because it is an attitude that appeals to concreteness, practicality, functionality, and the immediate effectiveness of explanations; religious, because it is cloaked in a dogmatic aura that, even when it does not convey spiritual themes, nevertheless takes on a definitive value.

In Snorri's tale, religious empiricism prevails at the end, neglecting the initial scene: the scene of violence. Loki's tales are steeped in violence, even the ties that bind him are made of the entrails of one of his sons, quartered by another whom the Aesir had mutated into a wolf; all this violence becomes a primitive lesson in geophysics. The hypothesis we intend to advance is that at the foundation of explanatory functionalism lies a violent scene, and that this scene is not only the building block of social bonding, as Girardian sacrificial theory claims, but also the social practice that constitutes and legitimizes knowledge and the sciences (Tomelleri, 2015). This epistemological circle will come in handy later.

The same pattern applies to play: the ethological functionalism whereby "A prepares B" tends to emphasize the evolutionary goal and neglect the predatory base from which it starts. While it is true that B is the diligent official in a business office, A is the carnivore preparing the ambush. The sweetening and mellowing of interpersonal relations becomes so demanding that it seems not only universal and necessary but also eternal and unchanging, only to break down suddenly when a quarrel breaks out between neighbors over an overly noisy dog, or perhaps when a superpower invades a neighboring state. In these moments of effervescence, the explanatory pattern fails and the evolutionary process is interrupted: one lives, literally, in a state of exception in which manners are suspended. B is no longer up to the situation; the official harnesses the machine gun like Michael Douglas in *Falling Down*; the mild-mannered mathematician initiates the massacre, like Dustin Hoffman in *Straw Dogs*.

The memory of the victim process fades, and, within the myth, ritual, and prohibition, distortions occur, aimed at rationalizing mythic practice and representation. In a sense, the work of misrecognition of the mythic religious and of ritual tends to be brought to completion by annulling the raison d'être of both myth and ritual. In this regard, writes René Girard, as a community moves away from the violent origins of its cult, the sense of ritual fades and moral dualism is strengthened.

On the level of practice, the rationalizing tendency acts either by softening prohibitions or by making rituals reasonable, or by doing both in combination. The system tends to unify under the aegis of a rationalization that does not correspond to its origin or raison d'être but leads ritual to attain an increasingly symbolic, abstract value, until it is replaced by the institution. For example, if rites of passage always succeed, if they regularly achieve their purpose, they gradually tend to turn into a simple rehearsal that becomes more and more symbolic as it becomes less and less random. The sacrificial element also tends to disappear, and one no longer knows what the symbol refers to.

Humans, in this way, have moved further and further away from the "essential violence" of "primitive" communities, the A dimension, according to our scheme, so much so that they lose sight of it once they become addicted to what they consider the universal and necessary outcome of civilization, that is, the B dimension. Although they never really break with violence, since it can still manifest itself in catastrophic forms today, according to Girard, the stereotype of violence has changed, precisely in relation to the process of symbolization. For us moderns, violence possesses a conceptual autonomy, a specificity, of which primitive societies have no idea. We primarily see the individual act, while primitive societies refuse to isolate it from its context, which is also perceived as violent.

This conceptualization of the stereotype of violence is the result, on the level of mythical representations, of the rationalizing distortion, which has both acted and continues to act in three different stages and according to an idealizing tendency, aimed at distinguishing good from evil. In the first stage, myth transcends the real and human origin of violence, relegating it to a divine realm, but the signs of violence and its collective unanimity still remain clear. The second stage involves the disappearance of collective violence and its replacement by individual violence. There follows a third stage, which involves suppressing even individual violence. In the terms of the play, we could say that there is a gradual move from violence to joking to mime to the synthetic gesture that no longer has anything explicitly violent about it. To some extent, this is what Norbert Elias calls the "civilizing process."

Let us explore, then, the first step. The god embodies the scourge: he does not stand beyond good and evil, but on this side. The god does not specify moral differences, and the transcendence of the victim has not yet fragmented into a good and divine power on the one hand, or an evil and demonic one on the other. In myth, the violence of collective murder is clearly depicted, and the violent action perfectly described, as in the case of the myth of Dionysus and the Titans in the Greek tradition. Girard writes: "In order to lure little Dionysus into their circle, the Titans shake certain trinkets. Seduced by these glittering objects, the child steps forward and the monstrous circle closes in on him. All at once the Titans murder Dionysus; after which they cook and devour him. Zeus, father of Dionysus, fulminates the Titans and resurrects his son." Only from the stage at which the difference between good and evil is actualized can the equivocal primitive deity split into a good hero and a monster that ravages the community: Saint George and the dragon. The monster embodies evil and therefore the one who kills (sacrifices) it is the hero. Even at this level, in any case, there is an initial rationalization, when the crimes of the god-victim are presented as unintended.

In the second stage, the myths visibly avoid defining an absolutely central scene as collective murder, which indeed demands such a definition. This scene is always presented in the same way—the murderers in a circle around their victim—but it substitutes for the murder other meanings, which share only the characteristic of not signaling the collective murder itself. The quoted scene from Snorri's *Edda* is a typical example of this procedure: this myth seems to be quite similar to the description of a collective murder, except for the trick of Baldr's invulnerability, which turns the description of the murder into a harmless game. Subsequently, the blame is polarized onto a single character, Loki, who uses the hand of a blind man, the naive Hödhr. In this way, the community of gods hides their guilt behind Loki's petty act.

There are several methods in mythology to reduce the guilt of the gods without laying it on the violent community and without, above all, revealing the victimizing process (Crow, 2018). We can summaries them into three main types: the second-degree scapegoat, the rascally god, and the angry god.

Girard, in referring to the second-degree scapegoat, means that mythical figure that arises from a reworking of the original myth. In the aforementioned myth, Loki, as the actual victim of the collective murder that originated the myth, is as innocent as Baldr, but to satisfy the idealizing tendency, which wants evil on the one hand and good on the other, he is indirectly blamed for the murder for which the whole community is responsible (the same can be said of the banquet version; Loki's torture is "justified" by the nefarious deeds he performs). With Loki, we are also in the presence of a type of deity that relates to the trickster; the god's action is conditioned by a misunderstanding, or the god appears to sometimes be so clever, or sometimes so stupid and clumsy, that he performs actions that compromise his mission yet at the same time ensure its success. In the myth of Cadmus, Cadmus himself may appear as a kind of rascally god when he throws the stone among the warriors: first, he causes the crisis by sowing the dragon's teeth; later through trickery, namely the deception of throwing the stone, he saves the Theban community, causing the death of all the warriors. The god is evil in jest.

Another way in which to dull the violence is when the effectively good god temporarily turns into a bad god because of a provocation from his community. In this way, disorder becomes the advocate of order: it is divine wrath that restores order. In the Loki tales, it is often Thorr who fills this role (in the Poetic *Edda*, Loki leaves Aegir's banquet only as a result of Thorr's threats). In this regard, Girard points out how the theology of wrath approaches the truth, but still remains imprisoned within the persecutory representation. For while the community divides the blame for the disorder between itself and the god and begins to take responsibility for its own unrest, only the action of the angry god restores order within the community.

The third stage of the rationalization process brings to completion what was left hanging in the first stage: the erasure not only of collective murder but also of violence itself. Emblematic here is the myth of Zeus's birth. His mother Rhea, in order to protect her newborn son Zeus from his father Kronos, who devours his own children, entrusts the infant, among others, to the Curets, minor deities who are part of her retinue, with the features of warriors. The terrified little Zeus begins to cry, and the Curets, to cover the noise of the cries, clash their weapons and behave in the loudest and most threatening manner possible. Arranged in a circle, the Curets remind us of the configuration and behavior of collective murder. However, violent action is entirely absent in this myth.

Collective violence is the core of the mythological machine, the device used to construct myths, sealed by the formula "A prepares B" and covered by the three layers of rationalization.

2.3. Envy and Paranoia

Back to the game. The scene from which we began was that of harmony interrupted by the spitefulness of the party pooper. We had wondered if there was an evolutionary reason for this strange phenomenon, and we had observed that functional explanations do not exhaust the mystery that transforms a pleasant experience into a possible nightmare; after all, the trickster's irruption is itself a manifestation of the presence of evil in the world, and as such cannot be rubricated merely as a faulty wheel in the complex gear of history or nature. Certainly, it is possible to enclose evil in a conceptual framework, to resolve it as a death drive (Freud, 1914), aggression (Lorenz, 1963), or domination of power (Canetti, 1960; Mishra 2017), but in any case we must recognize a gap of inexplicability, well expressed in myth when it presents the human vicissitude in its crudity devoid of moralism. But myth itself, manifesting mystery, at the very moment it presents it, is driven to disguise and conceal it: The victim becomes guilty. The pain is justified, the violence legitimate, or the disturbance consistent with the laws of nature.

Perhaps, however, rather than aspiring to the synthesis of an explanatory principle, it is worth clearly describing the way in which these destructive behaviors manifest themselves; indeed, this way is very often that of envy. Loki is evidently an envious character in both tales (toward the efficient servant, toward the munificent host . . .), and like him countless other evil characters in fairy tales or in modern myths of superheroes: think of the witch in *Sleeping Beauty*, envious of the social harmony of the small kingdom from which she feels excluded; or Snow White's stepmother, envious of her stepdaughter's beauty and youth; or even Magneto, the villain of the *X-Men* saga, envious of "normalcy"; or Green Goblin, envious of happiness.

The party pooper spoils the game by acting with envy, enacting a dynamic of desire ("I want to play too!") that, paradoxically, creates the system from which he feels excluded ("They won't let me play!"). Here, the "A prepares B" pattern is skipped. There is no "disliked" child (A) to provoke an exclusion procedure (B); play is established as a system capable of recognizing the excluded and legitimizing their exclusion. To fully understand this passage, however, we need to investigate the emotion characteristic of envy that we call the feeling of persecution, which classical psychiatry has called paranoia.

Paranoia is a typically Greek linguistic construct, like one of its close relatives, paradox. Paranoia circumvents the nous, and paradox circumvents the *doxa*; the former is synonymous with madness in the ancient world, while the latter is a rhetorical device that is highly useful in oratory. Aristotle, in the *Sophistical Refutations* (12), explains the function of this device in extreme summary: "As for proving that the interlocutor says something false and reducing the discourse to paradox (such in fact is the second end that sophistry proposes), it must be premised that this result is achieved through a certain way of conducting the inquiry and by means of the form of questioning." In some ways, it could be said that to reduce a discourse to paradox is to induce paranoia in the interlocutor. Refutation, which is the main art of the sophist, uses this means to confuse, stun, or silence their opponent. It is therefore no coincidence that the term "paranoia" has become, with the modern age, a very uncomfortable character in psychopathology, if only because of that semantic excess it carries with it, that over-meaning thereof. Paranoia is madness; fitting it into a psychiatric discourse thus becomes an arduous task.

The first obstacle is posed by classical psychiatric nosography; according to Emil Kraepelin, in fact, madness coincides with mental illness, and as such is defined as dementia praecox, or at the limit as manic depression, or circular disorder, which would later take on other names—for example, schizophrenia, bipolar disorder, and depression. Kraepelin's problem is where to place paranoia. There is no doubt that it is a mental illness; after all, Kraepelin is a psychiatrist, that is, a doctor of the psyche: what else can he see but mental illness? However, assuming it fits into the catalogue of mental illnesses, how can one reconcile the fundamental positivistic idea—not to say ideology—that mental illness concerns first and foremost cognitive degeneration (dementia), or at the limit mood abatement, with this bizarre disorder that does not involve the annihilation of intellectual abilities? Indeed, nor does paranoia necessarily induce depressive states.

Kraepelin is an architect of nosography; his edifice must be harmonious and balanced, making good with irregularities and disorders. For him, mental illness must coincide with dementia; non-demented delirium is a contradiction that can hold true only if it is a chronic condition. Delirium that is accompanied by the maintenance of lucid, conscious thought and that does not evolve into dementia is something inconsistent with Kraepelin's nosological framework, centered around the intellectual dimension.

The problem with paranoia is the role of thought. Just as the sophists could play with platitudes—the *doxas* use platitudes with great skill—in the same way, the paranoid eschew shared judgments, albeit using thought correctly. One can mock delirium ad libitum, but one cannot refute it because it is not an error of thought, but errant thoughts; it is not a trick but a deviation outside the norm. It is a paranormal experience. The problem with paranoia is not delirium as disorganized content, but rather its unquestionability.

Another important attempt at nosological synthesis, with far more fruitful outcomes, is that of Karl Jaspers, who, in order to explain delirium, distinguishes between *Wirklichkeit* and *Realität*, two terms that can be translated into English as "reality," but that refer to two very different roots. The former contains the noun *Wirkung*, "effect," so it is a sign of actual reality, which has effects and happenings with a world that transcends it. The latter is essence of res, so it is reality experienced idiosyncratically. What makes paranoid delirium a specific object of psychotherapy is not the remoteness from the "straight path" of reasoning, but rather the desperate loneliness forced upon the experiencing subject, what Ludwig Binswanger called the paranoid *Verweltlichung*: delirium becomes the world. It is not an opinion that can be argued about endlessly; it is nous made flesh and affect.

What the classical psychiatric approach lacks, however, emerges for the first time perhaps only with Freud, in the 1911 case of Judge Schreber; the case is arcane and paradigmatic of what Freud himself calls "paranoia." Indeed, Lacan (1958) posited this writing as an occasion for a radical reconstruction of the entire psychoanalytic framework. Consequently, we will not extensively dwell on the subject, except to highlight the novelty represented by the Freudian lens and the subsequent drifts that have formed from it. The novelty of psychoanalysis, at least in this truly fundamental case, consists of considering the patient's point of view as the starting point for diagnosis and treatment. What today seems taken for granted must have sounded like a kind of gross naiveté, or something out of tune to the ears of Kraepelin and Bleuer. Put simply, classical psychiatry never took into account the words of the insane. Psychoanalysis, on the other hand, listens to them for the first time.

Reading Schreber's memoir, Freud famously interprets the judge's hallucinations and delusions as projections of repressed homosexual desire. But before this controversial conclusion, Freud makes a very useful summary of what we shall try to define as the feeling of persecution, starting with a fundamental psychoanalytic principle, that of projection: "The study of several cases of delirium with a persecutory content has led me and many other scholars to believe that the relation between patient and persecutor can be brought back to a simple formula. . . . The main purpose of the persecution, of which the patient claims to be the object, is to justify such a change in emotional attitude" (Freud, 1911).

The Freudian "simple formula" has now become a passe-partout: Projection! Nevertheless, here in flagrancy, the interpretive dimension takes on a remarkable significance, if only because of the attention devoted to subjective experience and its emotional-affective content. Freud applies this pattern to the dynamics of desire; Schreber feels attraction for his physician, Flechsig, and transforms this "feminine fantasy" into "disdainful repudiation" by means of a "true masculine protest"; "The scantling cause of his illness thus consisted in an outburst of homosexual libido, the target of which was, probably from the beginning, Flechsig himself" (Freud, 1911).

The Freudian study of the Schreber case is particularly enlightening when attempting to understand the epistemological mechanism of understanding human behavior: Freud, who is to be credited with having paid unprecedented attention to what hitherto seemed to be nonsensical ramblings, seems more concerned with adapting the elements of the judge's autobiography to his own interpretive scheme; the power of the psychoanalytic paradigm prompts its founder to dare an "Aristotelian" application, to infer the particular from the universal of libidinal drives. Freud, however, does not dare to reverse this application—specifically, to induce the collected individual elements toward a larger pattern—evidently because in all likelihood there would be no pattern to contemplate at the end of the operation.

One of the recurring themes of Schreber's delusional ideas related to the stars, of which he was an excellent connoisseur, and from which he felt he came; he took refuge among the stars to defend himself from the cadaverous mass with which planet Earth was beset. Elias Canetti saw in this apocalyptic fresco the "sense of the position of the paranoid"—to stand high above others (Canetti, 1960). Paranoia, for Canetti, is a disease of power:

> Paranoia is *an illness of power* in the most literal sense of the words, and exploration of this illness uncovers clues to the nature of power clearer and more complete than those which can be obtained in any other way. One should not allow oneself to be confused by the fact that, in a case such as Schreber's, the paranoiac never actually attained the monstrous position he hungered for. Others have attained it. Some of them have succeeded in covering the traces of their rise and keeping their perfected system secret. Others have been less fortunate or had too little time. Here, as in other things, success depends entirely on accidents. The attempt to reconstruct these accidents under the illusion that they are governed by laws calls itself history. For every great name in history a hundred others might have been substituted. There is never any dearth of men who are both talented and wicked. Nor can we deny that we all eat and that each of us has grown strong on the bodies of innumerable animals. Here each of us is a king in a field

of corpses. A conscientious investigation of power must ignore success. We must look for its attributes and their perversions wherever they appear, and then compare them. A madman, helpless, outcast, and despised, who drags out a twilight existence in some asylum, may, through the insights he procures us, prove more important than Hitler or Napoleon, illuminating for mankind its curse and its masters. (Canetti, 1960, p. 448)

The feeling of persecution that torments the paranoid is also secondary for Canetti. Primary is the desire; this is not of an erotic-pulsional kind, but of power: the paranoid feels constantly surrounded by a secret mute whose true nature only they, with the "penetrating spiritual energy" with which they are endowed, can grasp. Freud, according to Canetti, is wholly incorrect in linking paranoia to homosexual desire, since the focus of Schreber's delusional ideas does not concern the libidinal sphere, but the intellectual one. Schreber feels attacks on his intellect everywhere, with every cosmic power aimed at preventing him from reasoning—every vision, every voice aimed at extinguishing the light of reason. Therefore, he defends himself by counterattacking or seeking, in absolute silence, stillness as freedom from words.

In Canetti's reading, there is an equally important element that needs to be highlighted in order to arrange the pieces of paranoia; in spite of the vividness of the visual and auditory hallucinations, in spite of the complexity of the illustrious paranoid's delusional picture, his disorder, Canetti argues, can be likened to "an atrophy of metamorphosis." The unmasking process to which the paranoid obsessively devotes himself, who is able to recognize the threat everywhere, is a process of antimutation, the opposite of metamorphosis. The paranoid is "absolutely unchanging." This is likely one of the fundamental differences between *dia-noia* (the intellect that transitions from one judgment to another) and *para-noia* (the intellect that discards), while the traversal of judgments drives the *noesis* to change form (premise, hypothesis, conclusion), discarding it places it motionless at the center of a circular configuration, of which it is able to grasp every element with a panoptic gaze. The fulcrum of a universal wheel, paranoia reveals itself to be an overt and meticulous art of grasping the sign of evil. The paranoid constantly wears the glasses of John Nada, the protagonist of John Carpenter's *They Live* (1988), who is able to see the monstrous aliens hidden among ordinary people. The doubter searches, changes his position, adapts, and moves from one point to another. The paranoid stands firm and does not doubt; he simply knows.

Now, if classical psychiatry rubricated paranoia among mental illnesses more or less forcibly but nevertheless unequivocally, if Freud recognized in it a projective system of repressed desires, if Canetti discerned in it the apotheosis of power over the masses, what is completely missing from each of these readings is an immanent element, almost trivial, as trivial as any phenomenon of historical reality, and above all leibhaft, of flesh, as is every true experience. Morton Schatzman's (1973) thesis concludes that underlying the feeling of persecution from which Schreber suffered was an actual experience of persecution suffered at the hands of his father, a well-known physician and pedagogue of the time, Daniel Gottlieb Moritz Schreber.

The point marked by Schatzman is stark and in some ways revolutionary; it bears a strong resemblance to the early Girardian analyses of the victimhood mechanism. There, too, it was a matter of highlighting an immanent, almost banal object, as trivial as any phenomenon of historical reality: the victim in the flesh (Girard, 1972). Daniel Paul Schreber's father was a kind of torturer, not unlike the great mass of fathers of his era (the nineteenth century) and his milieu (the Prussian upper middle class), only more methodical and systematic. His was a kind of shared normality, just as hyper-consumption is shared today; his son's departure from the groove he traced is analogous to the drug or alcohol high of today's well-bred teenagers. Schreber, a member of good society of his time, goes "off the deep end" (this effectively means "paranoia") because he was systematically subjected to harassment, torture, humiliation, and violence by his father. This is Schatzman's thesis. Here, it is necessary to pause in order to understand the reality of persecution.

Let us closely consider Schatzman's interpretive scheme. It is a nine-step path, an ennead of delusion. 1) The parent persecutes the child; 2) The parent sees his or her own persecution as love; 3) The child sees the parent's persecution as persecution; 4) The child (usually) does not understand that the parent understands the child's persecution as love; 5) The parent wants the child to love, honor, and obey the parent for the sake of the child. If the child does not do so, the parent must force the child to do so, for the child's sake; 6) The more the child sees the parent's persecution as persecution, the more the parent persecutes the child and sees their own persecution as love; 7) The child tries to hide the fact that they see the parent's persecution as persecution and to hide the fact that they are hiding something. The parent says to the child, "Dishonesty is bad. So I will punish you for your own good if you lie!"; 8) The child realizes that the parent will persecute them, especially if the parent sees that the child sees the parent's persecution as persecution and hides it and hides that there is something they are hiding; 9) The child hides from themselves that they see the parent persecuting them and hides from themselves that there is something they are hiding (Schatzman, 1973).

Schatzman's scheme, like many other theoretical and applied productions between the 1960s and 1980s, on the one hand, recalls the structure of the Batesonian double bind in terms of its epistemological framework (Bateson et al. 1956); on the other, it is proposed as a radicalization of a conflict with an environment (in this case, the familiar, bourgeois environment, the great defendant of the counterculture of the time) and with norms (manners and generational relationship). This radicalization is perhaps the least interesting aspect of Schatzman's reading, the one inevitably most exposed to the ravages of time. Instead, what should be over-emphasized is the manifestation of the actual reality of persecution as an explanatory principle not already of a distinct nosological dimension (as much as Schatzman is industrious in linking the gymnastic and orthopedic tortures of Schreber senior to the hallucinations of Schreber junior), but of a widespread malaise, a malaise of modernity, involving the healthy and the sick.

Much of the discussion about paranoia, as well as much of the discussion about schizophrenia, is actually a discussion about the definition of this term. Perhaps it should not be used at all. If its meaning were taken literally, it might apply validly to some individuals living alongside those to whom it is currently applied.

2.4. Play and Violence

Common sense holds that play and violence are two separate and disjointed systems. In reality, as we have seen, the relationship between play and violence is one of co-implication and co-evolution. The generative violence of the feeling of persecution is not an exception, an unsuccessful appendage of sociality; on the contrary, it is precisely through violence that the possibility of play is constructed. The same dynamic concerns what psychoanalysts call the object relation; there is no desire without envy, and vice versa. Envy reveals the reality of desire, just as the latter generates the possibility of converting motion toward the object into resentment toward those who undertake it (Tomelleri, 2015; Cohen, 2019).

A high example of this consubstantiality between play and violence and between envy and desire comes from none other than the Gospel. Chapter 9 of Mark's Gospel is packed with events. It begins with the famous episode of the transfiguration, in which Jesus shows his divinity to Peter, James, and John; then, after a discussion of the function of the prophets, there is a scene of exorcism: A young man possessed by a powerful demon suffers convulsions. Jesus casts out the demon and, as is often the case, commands that the news of what has happened not be spread. The disciples are bewildered, arguing among themselves about who is the greatest, and Jesus rebukes them: "Anyone who wants to be first must be the very last, and the servant of all." (Mark 9:35). Immediately after, the theme of exorcism returns, but this time it is envy that takes over. Let us follow the text:

> John said to him, "Teacher, we saw someone driving out demons in your name and we told him to stop, because he was not one of us." But Jesus said, "Do not stop him, for no one who does a miracle in my name can in the next moment say anything bad about me, for whoever is not against us is for us. Truly I tell you, anyone who gives you a cup of water in my name because you belong to the Messiah will certainly not lose their reward." (Mark 9:38–41)

Jesus has just uttered one of his most famous phrases: embracing a child, he says, "Whoever welcomes one of these little children in my name welcomes me" (Mark 9:37), and immediately John, the beloved apostle, provokes him by bringing the conversation back to a topic that was haunting the Twelve. Is their condition privileged? Does the fact that they belong to the retinue of the Messiah's intimates make them more powerful people than the rest of the world? And among them, are some more powerful than others? Let us not forget that these reflections shortly follow the transfiguration, which is a moment of extreme revelation accorded only to three chosen ones. Envy irrigates every line of this chapter. John seems not to be holding up any longer; we saw, he says, a man practicing exorcisms and, we syooise he even succeeded! Otherwise we cannot explain the outrage. Well, we stopped him because "he was not of us."

The apostle John provides an illuminating example of the mechanism of envy; the object is "casting out demons." This is a highly complex object, about which so much could be said, but this is not the place. Let us hold on to exorcism as the object of desire. Jesus is the one who is able to cast out demons; indeed, in the very chapter we are reading, he shows that he is the best at it, so much so that his followers ask him why they cannot and he can. Jesus evidently has means that others lack. This difference generates desire (*I want to be like him*) and envy (*I want to have what he has*). Jesus very often tries to defuse envy through service: It is not about having some power but rather about getting all power out of the way. It is not about commanding but about serving. It is not about excelling but about becoming humble, already learning not to take but to ask (i.e., to pray). But for the apostles, these messages are too complicated. Envy, on the other hand, is very simple. In fact, as soon as someone shows that they can juggle exorcism with naive familiarity, they are immediately stopped, because they have not done the groundwork, if you can call it that, have not followed all the procedures, do not meet the selection criteria, are "not of ours."

The object—casting out demons—is no longer such; it, as happens when anything is invested with desire, reveals its relational nature. What is at stake is not the object per se, the exorcism, but what it implies: power, primacy, precedence. Jesus realizes this passage. In fact, he does not reiterate the prerogative over the object. He does not say "only I can cast out demons." Instead, he emphasizes the relationship. In doing so, he emphasizes the paranoid motive of envy, which moves forces in a centripetal direction, is interrupted by the motive of charity. He who does good cannot harm, and he who does good does good to all.

As can be seen from this example, envy and desire move in the same field. The same is true of play and violence; play and violence are not two different forces, but two vectors of the same force. They sometimes travel in divergent directions, but at other times their trajectories intersect until they merge into each other. When the balances break down, play ceases to be play, and violence takes over. There is no original dimension of play that is devoid of violence; just as there is no object of desire incapable of generating envy. Relationship precedes, as Bateson says, the inertia of things. And while relationship can be pleasant and joyful, it can also be painful and charged with anger.

We could say that a simple form of playful relationship is the race. Competition, as a form of play, is an end in itself; however, in competitions there is a winner and a loser. Victory is extraneous to the competition itself; it is a goal substantially different from the practice that constitutes the competition. However, even just the prestige enjoyed by the winner increases the participants' willingness to engage in the competition. The presence of an audience, of a third-party gaze that legitimizes and enhances the competition, makes the stakes increasingly valuable. Think of when we go fishing: if we are alone and catch a large fish, our joy will be limited to the achievement of a possibly unhoped-for goal; but if we are in company, and others praise us for our prowess, the satisfaction will be much greater!

Now, a particularly interesting form of a race that can help us accurately describe the game in its relation to violence is what Johan Huizinga (1938/2002) calls the "race of insults." The Dutch historian reports the case of some pre-Islamic tribes that engaged in such contests, called *mufākhara*: two clans meet and engage in a challenge, entrusting their spokesmen, often the poets representing the family group, with the task of singing the praises of their own lineage and insulting that of others. Insult contests are also present in the Greek tradition, on which satirical poetry is based, and in the Germanic tradition, of which we have seen, in the song of Loki, a fairly typical example. But in times much closer to our own, we can mention freestyle competitions.

The contest is such when the playful dimension prevails over the violent one; in insulting contests, the aim is not to tell the truth about the other, but to create the most surprising juxtaposition, the most shocking insult. In the game, there is no ambition for truth, which is instead triggered the moment violence overpowers it. When the metaphor ceases to be a metaphor and becomes a literal definition, the mechanism of the game jams, and violence breaches the relationship. But again it must be reiterated that this is not a different force; in the same system, play and violence, like desire and envy, pleasure and pain, cohabit, constituting an indissoluble pair, a kind of yin and yang of sociality.

For this reason, it is not only possible but also extremely useful to investigate play not so much as a premise of a subsequent serious reality, according to the "A prepares B" scheme, but as a social reality already in place, already containing every possibility and every destiny. For this, moreover, it is not only possible but also extremely useful to play and to watch others play, reflecting on their own and others' styles. In this way, one can realize the potential of a science, sociology, which is not abstracted from its subject matter, but is rather innervated by it and embodies, in its epistemological structure, the relational dynamics it seeks to explain and describe. This is what it means, after all, to play sociology.

CHAPTER 3

Sympathy for Play

WE HAVE SEEN HOW SYMPATHY IS A DECISIVE ELEMENT IN UNDERstanding the dynamics of play. The term sympathy, of course, is by no means unambiguous. Today it is used as indiscriminately—and misleadingly—to the point of becoming a kind of social commandment or codified obligation in public relations: in a manner analogous to the imperative of *jouissance*, which characterizes the "discourse of the capitalist" (Lacan, 1978), "sympathy" is the mask, paradoxically, of its opposite, which is not antipathy but apathy, the "sad passion" of indifference (Zamperini, 2007). The obligation to be likeable in marketing matches the sympathy for the devil of the transgressive trend of the day. To be likeable or dislikeable today is synonymous with the assumption of a posthumous surrogate that takes the place of the actual social bond in agony. Therefore, in advanced societies like ours, gestures and expressions of sympathy do not necessarily correspond to a real and widespread emotion, but may be the outcome of an anthropological perversion; for example, shaking hands and smiling have nothing to do with sharing an experience or feeling. If sympathy becomes the object of prescription, it is no longer such. Clearly, we are not dealing with this eventuality here, but it is appropriate to make explicit the concern due to the semantic drift of a term that, in itself, is indicative of a relational dynamic: sympathy, in fact, as far as we are concerned, is the pathos that binds, the consideration of the other's gaze. Then again, even play is necessarily imprescriptible, sharing with sympathy at least a matrix of genuine freedom. It is on this that we will now have to dwell.

3.1. A Secret Feeling

The gaze of the other establishes the possibility of play in simply taking into account the behavior of others. The very idea of the rule of play depends on generic and superficial signs of approval and disapproval in a seamless bond. There is undoubtedly a wholly human capacity to "feel the other," without necessarily sharing their feelings and emotions. This capacity, studied mostly from a psychodynamic or phenomenological perspective, is indeed the core of social bonding, and it is rather bizarre that it has been largely neglected by the social sciences. In any case, as we have seen, the notion of sympathy, which for Darwin constitutes the key element in describing elementary relational processes, is originally taken from Adam Smith's *Theory of Moral Sentiments* (1759/2006), a work in which he analyzes the fundamental criteria by which to judge and classify social actions. From this pioneering investigation, we will find the cue for a sociological reflection on play, that is, for a type of interpretation that accounts for the irreducibly social nature of playful actions.

Smith's starting point is represented by the central assertion of Rousseau's *Discourse on the Origin of Inequality* (1755) that humanity begins the moment we begin to evaluate the gaze of others. All judgment of an action and all motivation to act, according to Smith, take shape only through relationship with others: "Whatever judgment we can form . . . it must always bear some secret reference, either to what is, or to what, upon a certain condition, would be, or to what, we imagine, ought to be, the judgment of others" (Smith, 1759/2006, p. 99). This "secret reference" to the judgment (actual or imagined) of others is at the very heart of social bonding. It is most important that Smith notes both the "secrecy" of the dynamic and the fact that this process is triggered regardless of the actual presence of judgment. This is precisely what sympathy is: It is secret, since it precedes awareness. It is somehow the unconscious side of social life, and it is intimately disinterested, insofar as the gaze of the other is sought even where it is not, just as the judgment of others is presupposed even when it is not given.

From this point of view, the figure of Smith is presented in a new light compared to the more widespread utilitarian image, due more to the reception of the *Inquiry into the Nature and Causes of the Wealth of Nations* (1776). In sharp contrast to the rational-utilitarian reading, Smith abandons the idea that there can exist in man a self-love, a "self-love" rooted in an individuality understood as self-sufficient and fulfilled. Self-love is merely a way of securing the consideration of others. The Smithian subject is radically unfulfilled because he cannot do without the gaze of others: he has an almost desperate need for his fellow human beings to forge an identity for himself (Dupuy, 1992). Smith's utilitarian image does not hold up to a reading of the *Theory of Moral Sentiments* based entirely on the idea that sympathy governs human relationships according to a relational mode, characterized by a reflexive logic, that puts any utilitarian principle in the background. Even where the Smithian individual appears to be pursuing his or her own exclusive self-interest, this strategy serves only to gain the recognition of others. Imagining the judgment of others, a social practice of inestimable versatility, as Gregory Bateson and Richard Wright Mills, among others, will grasp, involves the ability to consider the moral and social principles that govern relationships, which in turn originate in relationships. "In the beginning is the relation": this is not only a famous motto (Buber, 1923/2013), more or less, but also a fundamental epistemological condition.

In order to define sociological games, it is indispensable to delve into this condition: for if moral principles and norms emerge from relational practices based on sympathy, this means that there are not, "in the beginning," absolute principles or values, such that by deduction one arrives at concrete, singular experiences. Rather, it is the opposite: that is, it is social relations that induce the formulation of norms or principles. But these relations, "in the beginning," are precisely games. It is by playing, in fact, that we first pool the ability to exchange looks, judgments, and values with one another. If in the beginning is the relationship, then, that "initial" relationship is the game.

We have seen how, in Smith, self-love is ostensibly a quality of the individual, but it actually stems from the desire for mutual recognition. At the basis of human relationships is not the selfish individual driven by the utilitarian principle of "self-love": self-love is inscribed in an interplay of reciprocities generative of the social bond.

The gaze of the other, or rather the need to be recognized that is expressed through the "secret reference" to the other's face, takes on considerable depth in Smith: it becomes an "impartial and well-informed spectator" (Smith, 1759/2006, p. 115). This spectator is almost identical to what almost two centuries later George Herbert Mead would call the "generalized other" (Mead, 1934). When in common parlance we speak of conscience, from whose "voice" the suggestions to act well should come, we merely conjure up the image of a perfect man (this means "impartial and well-informed"), who in turn personifies the "secret referral" to the other.

The notion of sympathy outlined in this way has nothing to do with "good feelings": there is nothing edifying, per se, in identifying the meeting place of micro- and macrosocial dynamics, the middle ground between the public and the private, which is the ability to grasp or imagine the other's approval or disapproval. Just as at the beginning of the chapter we saw fit to distinguish the idea of sympathy from its instrumentalization, its globalized merchandizing, it is now appropriate to clear the field of moralistic or consolatory temptations. Sympathy is not a "good feeling" (Dupuy, 1992, 2016).

Outlined in this way, the notion of sympathy, as we have seen, constitutes the deep nexus between individual and group. In the perspective of play, this function turns out to be decisive: for if we consider the process of play in all its breadth, it must be seen that the initiation of play belongs as much to the individual sphere as to the collective sphere, and to neither of them in an exclusive and dominant way. Play, as a radical form of social relation, leveraging sympathy, is a singular and plural experience. To grasp this paradoxical condition, this original relation (Nancy, 1996), it is necessary to look more closely at the terms in question.

3.2. Two Ways (at least) to Say *Game*

There is more than one way to say something: this obvious observation, handed down from Aristotle, concerning being—*pollachos legomenon*, "is said in many ways"—is not at all obvious if we consider it carefully, especially if we apply it to relations. Bateson noted how there are at least two distinct languages for talking about our interactions: the first language is the one that describes the psychology of an individual (and is perhaps the one most widely used and accredited); the second is the one that describes relationships between individuals. These two languages are not mutually exclusive, but imply each other according to a complementary logic (Bateson, 1960). For example, the language of psychology describes as an "internal state," the wagging of a dog's tail, but this same language says nothing about the relationship this dog has with its owner at the moment it sees him. Wag, indeed, is said in many ways and so much more so playing.

But let us proceed step by step. For individualistic psychology, expression makes "public" what the individual feels in "private"; it therefore becomes a system of signals that informs about a subject's hidden state. Once again a concealment: before there was the "secret" referral to the other's judgment, according to Adam Smith's brilliant insight, now we have a hidden content that is somehow revealed through expression. In fact, this is the way we usually think our feeling and knowing of the world "works." That is, we think there is something "inner" that, depending on various factors (age, social background, culture, education, etc.), we may or may not decide to bring out. The discourse of the language of "inner states" does indeed refer back to the most common sense ways of thinking. But it is not the only one.

In the previous chapter, we described this sort of "game of pretenses" represented by language based on internal-external dualism and the idea that a social scientist's units of analysis are individuals. The assumptions of such attitudes may themselves be ontological or methodological; in the former case, this way of describing social action is considered the only one that adequately corresponds to reality; in the latter, it depends on a contingent choice of the observer. Let us therefore put this multiplicity of languages to the test.

Let us observe a game in its initial moment: four kindergarten children start walking in the courtyard holding each other arm in arm and exclaiming in chorus, in a very loud and almost sing-songy voice, "Who wants to play wolf?" Gradually other children join the initial group, until an adequate number is reached (nine children), and then the game can begin, although it often happens that children take longer to set up the game and complicate it, than to actually play.

Now, if we consider the two languages that Bateson spoke of, we find that here we are dealing both with defining a series of individual behaviors, the sum of which produces the organization of the little group that wants to play wolf, and with describing a complex relationship, a dynamic process, a growth in terms of numbers (the children going from four to nine) and in terms of relationships. The signal of walking arm in arm and inviting other playmates with a standard formula is quite explicit; however, there are details that remain in the shadows if we limit ourselves to examining the scene by taking into account only external signals as so many indices of "internal states," that is, using only individual-centered language. For example, how does the decision to join the group take place? How is the newcomer grafted into the small chain? And most importantly, who and how does one decide that's enough? If one does not take into account the language that describes relationships—that is, the social dimension of sympathy—one cannot come to grips with this complementary plane to individual psychologies. Thinking of interactions as mere approval/disapproval exchanges, that is, thinking in terms of inner individualistic language, works well, as we know, indeed it is the most convenient and widespread way of representing reality; however, it proves ineffective when questions arise about how procedures and interactions develop in a particular context.

Most theories of emotion and theories of rational play using the language of the psychology of the individual use the conceptual category of utility to answer these questions. From this perspective, an individual expresses a certain emotion because it is personally useful to him or her for whatever reason: evolutionary (adaptive advantage), social (work or status advantages), etc. Similarly, if this is the case, we play because, either biologically or socially, play produces conditions that are useful for the preservation of the species or the welfare of the community. However, we know well that these kinds of explanations are far from convincing (Huizinga, 1938/2002; Dumouchel, 1995). First, a question that has given rise to a very large polemical literature, what is really "useful"? And then, assuming even that one plays to derive some individual or group benefit, does playing end in its usefulness? And is the latter the motivational lever, whereby someone rationally decides to play for advantage?

In the face of these questions, the explanatory category of utility is highly problematic: the questions it solves are equal to those it opens. Anyone who has played has experienced the gratuitousness and futility of play and how enjoyable it is precisely for that reason. But the inner individualistic language, to return to Bateson's essay, is not the only one through which it is possible to explain affective life and its close connection with games of interaction. Another way is to focus on relationships, where the notion of "signal" takes on a very different meaning. Bateson's hypothesis is that in this case signals should be interpreted as referring not to internal states of the subject but to relational contingencies. In other words, a signal accommodates or proposes what will be the modalities of a relationship of which the subject is a part.

3.3. Cybernetics of Play

Bateson defines the notion of contingency through a particularly suggestive example:

> When you open the refrigerator door and the cat comes up and makes certain sounds, she is not talking about liver or milk, though you may know very well that that is what she wants. You may be able to guess correctly and give her that—if there is any in the refrigerator. What she actually says is something about the relationship between herself and you. If you translated her message into words, it would be something like, dependency, dependency, dependency. She is talking, in fact, about a rather abstract pattern within a relationship. From that assertion of a pattern, you are expected to go from the general to the specific—to deduce milk or liver. (1972, pp. 215–16)

When we express a feeling, we suggest a relationship of a certain kind to the other, and we expect the other to act on the basis of the relationship so suggested. Similarly, the dog wagging his tail does not merely express an internal state but proposes and sanctions a relational context between him and his master. Thus, walking arm in arm around the yard intoning "Who wants to play wolf?" opens up a contingency of relationships tuned, if you will, on play.

Assuming the second language—the one that describes relationships—gestures, movements, vocalizations, and facial expressions become signals that define inter-individual contingencies, telling us about the kind of relationship that exists between the participants of a given interactive game. These signals are usually nonverbal and invest only the affective dimension of human relationships; they are often emitted unconsciously and received equally unconsciously. The language of internal states and the language of relationships, in the social science tradition, have almost always been considered incompatible, reasoning that one had to be sacrificed in order to make the theory of the other consistent: thus it happened that game theory (and the very idea of sympathy) was traced solely to its more rigorously individualistic presupposition. In fact, when one speaks of game theory, one can only refer back to mathematical thinking; Nash equilibrium; von Neumann's zero-sum games; and probability dynamics in financial, political, or intelligence strategies. Which is quite a far cry from our children in the kindergarten playground. Game theory works as long as we reflect on the decisions of a single player, assuming that utility is the only parameter at play. But if we want to understand the play context and its relational implications, it is not enough.

Social action, as we have been able to see since the beginning of our investigation, is profoundly ambivalent, and this ambivalence requires to be interpreted in another way, through the necessary complementarities between intra-individual and inter-individual communicative dimensions. If one puts the question in relational terms, that is, if one chooses to talk about the expression of emotions and play through a language that foregrounds relationships, the problem is no longer to establish the utility, for the individual or for the species, of an action. It will be necessary if it can regulate the forms of the relational contexts in which subjects find themselves. And here comes back the "hidden" or "secret" aura that surrounds play, and which Bateson renders in his own right, when at the beginning of the October 1955 Macy Conference at Princeton, devoted precisely to play, he begins by pointing out the almost daunting elusiveness of his chosen topic, so much so that he states, "There is something like a 'not' implied in the word play" (Bateson, 1956).

What is this "not" implicit in play? It is, we might say, the hallmark of its ambivalence. Play *isn't* serious, *isn't* real, *isn't*—as Bateson provocatively puts it—a chair, etc. This negative definition of play is an interesting way to explain the virtue of the language of relations: for it does not aim at representation, but at the explication of the multiplicities of references implicit in the sign. If *being* (and, a fortiori, *play*) is said in many ways, it is worth dwelling on all of them, without pretending to reduce a complex practice to a reaction mechanism: "Through play an individual becomes aware of the existence of various types and categories of behavior" (Bateson, 1956).

But this is not just awareness training: play, when considered according to the language of relationship, reveals its exquisitely contextual nature. Play opens up contexts (Bateson would perhaps even say: universes). Children who, hearing the invitation to play wolf, join the group, adhere to an unspoken message, respond nonverbally to a nonverbal appeal, which is the soul and at the same time the engine of the play process: the message "this is a game." More often than not, this is an implicit message, which when verbalized perhaps sanctions the end of a game rather than its beginning, because reminding someone that a game is being played makes one think of some improper stroke. The impetuous lover who dares "borderline" caresses on the night of the first date knows this well, but so do martial arts enthusiasts, who when training get "hot" a little too much and risk getting a few black eyes. At some point you have to stop and say, "Hey, look it's for pretend!" or something like that. To explicate the message "this is a game" is, after all, to step outside the frame-context that the game has opened. While that message, like the hidden reminder of sympathy, is the secret core of all playful action. As long as it remains as such, play lives its magical equilibrium within which a meow, far from being a simple internal state signal, can mean many things.

Within this framework, deception and pretense also lose the problematic connotations they retain in the perspective of the psychology of the individual and acquire new meaning. Deception and pretense, "cheating," as we had already seen at the end of the previous chapter, become an integral part of the interactive dynamics, while the supposed evolutionary utility of the individual takes a back seat. The issue of cheating, not surprisingly, is one of the issues at the center of studies in sociobiology and rational choice theory, as well as, as we shall see shortly, in Goffmanian phenomenology.

According to Hamilton (1964), human beings are unique in their ability to lie to other members of their species and in a way that deliberately favors their own kinship and genetic heritage. Whether an animal can cheat a fellow animal from the perspective of evolutionary adaptation is as complex an issue as altruism. In both cases, an animal chooses to act toward another (by cheating or helping) out of adaptive convenience, in terms of overall genetic fitness. However, this explanation runs aground before the problem of figuring out how one can know in advance whether in a given, singular situation it is more convenient to be altruistic or deceitful with one's fellow animal.

From this emerges the fundamental importance of the relational contingency signals that Bateson speaks of: seeking the other's gaze, approval or disapproval, cannot be reduced to selfish or utilitarian "judgment," a posteriori, to a mere strategy to deceive or manipulate. We do not seek the other merely so that he or she will recognize or serve us; we seek him or her out of sympathy, that is, the interhuman dynamic that makes us social animals. This is a constitutive feature of the contingency of any interaction game. The signal conveying the message "this is a game" corresponds, in other words, to the "once upon a time" formula that opens the traditional fairy tale. In both cases, a ritual structure puts participants in agreement around what is not game and not fairy tale (Bruner, 2000).

Sympathetic relationships become the relational frame within which our actions, the "plays," take a certain emotional shape. A very rich literature related to role-playing and, especially in the United States, simulation games has developed on this framework (a few examples: Boockok & Coleman, 1966; Boockok & Shild, 1968; Taylor & Walford, 1972; Bondioli, 1996, Capranico, 1997; Angiolino, Giuliano & Sidoti, 2003), focused mainly on the definition of conduct and psycho-pedagogical designs. This strong emphasis on the educational scope of play, however, has ended up overshadowing what is probably the most important but therefore itself the least controllable element of play. Considering play as one of the many possibilities for expression and training; analyzing it according to the cognitive, emotional, and social skills of the subjects; applying it to specific educational and training programming; administering it as a palliative anti-stress cure, as a formula for warding off drop-outs, etc., all this is undoubtedly a testament to the importance of this social practice in the daily order of our experiences. But it is not enough. This approach risks disconnecting various relational styles and modes within so many separate boxes, satisfying the classificatory urge, which is a favorite game of social scientists but which does not go beyond a pure and sterile self-referentiality. The social dimension of play is in place long before classificatory distinctions, long before the rules of play themselves are defined: the arm-in-arm children evoking the wolf game are already in play, because they have already triggered the gaze game that constitutes the signal of relational contingency. Therefore, from a sociological point of view, distinguishing between fantasy play, simulation play, role-play, etc., is in some ways misleading. It may be most important on the level of psychodynamic study (Sroufe, 1995), but it says nothing about the relationships that are exercised and experienced when playing games.

The sociological perspective investigates the surface element of play, which is also the most intangible, perhaps precisely because it is arguably the most prevalent. That element, we have seen, is made of the same stuff of which gestures, grimaces, smiles, and the almost imperceptible movements of eyelashes and lips—the still unarticulated lines that precede an exchange of jokes, a challenge, or a surrender. What Erving Goffman (1969) called a "sub-area" of sociology is in effect our privileged field of inquiry and experimentation.

3.4. Face-to-Face

Perhaps no one has analyzed the minimal details of face-to-face interactions with such rigor and such astonishing attention as Goffman. For our part, we will try to follow in his footsteps by focusing in particular on the notion of immediacy (Kendon, 1988). When Goffman speaks of the "sub-area" of sociology, he does so with the stated intention of carving out a specific area of inquiry in which the inter-individual relationship is configured in the immediate, in the here and now. Immediacy seems to us to be an essential condition for the investigation of the game as well, since the relational context signal can only take place in the simultaneous presence of the players. (It is obvious that in virtual game situations, such as in communities where video game tournaments are organized, the face-to-face is diminished and replaced by a different immediacy, linked to the display and no longer to the face of the other, but this is something we cannot go into now.) The interaction that takes place in immediacy is precisely the field of events and forces in which the game can begin. For this it is necessary to dwell on Goffman and his perspicuous description of interaction. It is in fact Goffman who provides the most refined but at the same time the most ambiguous tools: more refined, because the Canadian sociologist is adept at highlighting the mute and unconscious drama that is staged in an intersection of glances, but also more ambiguous, because despite the immense wealth of details and particulars, Goffman's treatment takes us only to the threshold of our experience, that is, it prevents us from crossing the sub-area of interaction. Relationship, in fact, is something other than interaction. And yet the latter is an indispensable moment of the playful process and as such must be investigated.

The necessary condition for there to be interaction, it was said, is immediacy, the simultaneous presence of two actors, the vis-à-vis. Goffman speaks in this regard of the "mere presence" of individuals as a sufficient element to influence the environment. The advantage of analyzing situations of immediate interaction lies in the fact that direct observation makes accessible a considerable amount of information, which otherwise would not be available. The example Goffman provides, though incidental, is illuminating. Granted that every human being "exudes expressions" (p. 11), somewhat as in Watzlawick's well-worn first postulate, it is one thing to express such emotions by reading a letter, quite another to express them in front of the interlocutor, without mediation. The difference is abysmal, evidently, as we know well and perhaps even better than Goffman today, in the midst of the digital age, where millions of nicknames conceal age, gender, character, and personal desires. Nonetheless, even in its apparent triviality, this distinction is most important: the mediation of writing ("Gutenbergian" or electronic) does not prevent the expression of emotions, but it does make their recognition and understanding more arduous; whereas in face-to-face communication, interpretive efforts are minimized. Let it be said in passing, this reduction to the minimum is relative to the ability of the observer, which in Goffman's case was definitely above average; as Norbert Elias once said, Goffman was certainly a genius, but those who today attempt to move along the paths he traced find themselves burdened with "theoretical reflections" that he could afford to overlook: "Their observations lack freshness and are prone to sclerotize into formalistic constructs, driven by the need to force what is observable here and now into the straitjacket of some universal and axiomatic scheme" (1978/2009, p. 18).

We have thus seen how Goffman, in a lightning move, locates his field of inquiry in immediate interaction, distinguishing it from other forms of mediated contact with others. The face-to-face, as the generative of the social relationship, far from being an atom, that is, an indivisible entity, a point in the geometric sense of the term, is a complex and richly detailed process. It is a specifically human complexity, Goffman says, although it is not entirely absent in animals, that is, the fact that in any face-to-face situation one is not limited to expression to communicate: one speaks, one conveys information, one constructs messages, and "by definition the message is in a sense independent of the context and its content is by no means limited to the sender" (1969, p. 12).

This point is very important: on the one hand, Goffman is saying that there is a biological, universal matrix of interaction (whereby all organisms gather information from the environment), and, on the other hand, he is pointing out, in the human case, "instinct is not sufficient" (p. 17). That there is a mutuality between "mere presence" and interaction, or to put it better, between life and knowledge, is a revolutionary principle of the most up-to-date biology and an assumption of complexity epistemology (Varela, 1979; Maturana, 1988; Ceruti, 1986). From the sociological point of view, this is confirmed in the analysis of immediate interaction. But here Goffman adds something else, without, however, explaining it: where instincts are no longer sufficient, "deliberate self-conscious efforts are made to obtain information from what is happening in the immediate environment." In sum, Goffman argues that the basis of immediate interaction is common to all living organisms, while its "strategic" complexity is specifically human (or at least concerns "higher" organisms). Beyond the fact that the sciences of biological autonomy would disprove the assumption that self-consciousness is unrelated to the organism (Maturana, 1988), Goffman really seems to fall into a kind of contradiction, because he insists on focusing on a kind of sociological substratum that is the immediate face-to-face, and then argues that the communicative dimension, i.e., language, occurs on a higher plane, such that even the message is "in a sense independent of the context."

We need to explain this contradiction, because it concerns us very closely: if in fact play, as we have hypothesized, is the basis of the core of the relationship, that is, the nonverbal understanding that sanctions the message "this is a game," it is necessary that this basis is itself secure; that is, it is necessary that the epistemological approach and the sociological gaze that highlight and bring it to the fore are not characterized by fragile or inconsistent assumptions. In this regard, we must ask a question: what is immediate interaction made of? Or even: how does play unfold as an elementary practice? Is it a simple interweaving of glances and muted reciprocity, or is it something more complex, in which language and the transmission of information come into play?

It is Goffman himself who provides the key to answering this question and resolving the contradiction. In describing the "games of expressions," he distinguishes five "fundamental moves": the unintentional move, the naive move, the masking move, the unmasking move, and the counter-masking move. Of these five moves, we are particularly interested in the first two. The first, the unintentional move, corresponds roughly to "mere presence": in short, it is any behavior that acquires meaning only if it falls within a "game" (of which it knows nothing, evidently), that is, if it is observed by another. The mere presence of an observer evaluating the unintentional move constitutes the second move, the naive move, which occurs "when the observer thinks that the subject can be accepted for what it seems, that is, that he is making an unintentional move" (1969, p. 19).

The dynamic of these two moves closely resembles the Smithian principle of sympathy. There is here, too, a tension toward the other that undermines naive realism. Just as in Smith, the judgment of the other is sought regardless of his actual presence, so too in Goffman the naive move produces the unintentional move, even if the latter were only imagined, misunderstood, or even disguised. This is, in nuce, the game. It does not dwell in the "meta" dimension of the verbal symbol, yet neither is it an immediate dimension of interaction. There are always mediations, even, paradoxically, in immediacy; this is what Goffman does not make explicit but suggests through the contradiction between simple presence and communicative complexity.

However much we go about reducing the interactive exchange to the "minimum," still following Goffman, that is, isolating the area least compromised by interpretations and overdeterminations—and, for Goffman, the minimum is that the issuer has the capacity to communicate (p. 14)—we always find mediations that make the unintentional move ambivalent. That is, they make it potentially different from what it seems, they make it the beginning of a game. What is most interesting to us, from this perspective, is that, as Roger Caillois had intuited, there is not really a metaphysical origin of the game: the game begins when the unintentional move is observed by the naive move. In the beginning, there is no dimensionless point, but there is an imaginative investment that requires confirmation. Therefore, the second move creates the first, but not out of nothing, rather from a "simple presence" and comparison with a "generalized other" that provides the term of comparison for understanding the first. Which means that pure and simple interaction does not exist, there is never immediacy: every strategy requires some form of mediation. The generalized other, which is the "excluded third" in Goffman's reflection, the impersonal other of linguistics (Benveniste, 1966), is the guarantor of the social relation; it is what makes sure that there is the relation. The fact that its unexpected appearance causes a considerable disturbance is counter-evidence that the social relation is based on its removal. *Lupus in fabula* is the magic formula for chasing away the embarrassment of the excluded third party who suddenly shows up. And children who play wolf set out to find, with each other, a third party that they will always keep in the shadows as long as the game lasts. The wolf is the mask of the nascent state of the social relationship; it is one of many ways of saying the message "this is a game."

CHAPTER 4

Sociological Games

PLAY HAS AN AFFECTIVE, RELATIONAL, AND SOCIAL NATURE. ONE DOES not play merely because it is advantageous, or for gain of any kind (adaptive, therapeutic, educational, economic, etc.), but for the pleasure of play. Our species shares with other higher mammals a natural aptitude for play. Our hypothesis is that this aptitude precedes all other kinds of interaction. It is at one with our propensity for the other's gaze, sympathy, which is the original core of all playful activity. If play is the secret of social relationship, then it comes before everything else. There is play as an ethological and anthropological condition, but, on the sociological level, we only ever experience games situated in a historical and social context. Every society has its own games that can be classified in various ways. Sociological analysis is called upon to study the nexus between culture and play activities, to understand their functions and possible classifications, questioning how games contribute to the evolution or involution of social behavior. But there is also another way of treating games from a sociological point of view, namely, imagining them as simulated social contexts, where players enact society. The analysis here turns to the study of the production of subjectivity (identity, individual acting, groups, active minorities, etc.) and the production of structures (space, time, the body, resources, institutions, and organizations).

4.1. Playing Society

A sociological game is essentially a social positioning game. A player's main activity is to participate in activities with others, creating and orienting a distinctive and recognizable self-image. Enacting conducts, according to specific positional practices, means physically placing oneself within a space and at a specific time. At the same time, one's position serves as a differential measure; that is, it serves to construct the relationship with the place that others are occupying, without necessarily having thereby assumed a specific and definable social role within cultural repertoires. In short, simply occupying a space is enough to influence the course of action and play. Play begins simply when one decides to participate with others in an activity that one recognizes as play. This is a circularity that, as we have seen from Bateson's analyses, is constitutive of play itself.

Sociological games do not coincide with traditional role-playing. The role can be described as a predetermined point of interconnection between personal motivation and broader predefined normative and value frames. Take, for example, the role of the mayor. The mayor, in order to consolidate his political authority, uses, often unconsciously, ancient symbols of power and mystery, evocative language (demagogic, populist, politicalese, etc.), and "palace secrets," each of which is legitimized before the citizens in terms of functionality and efficiency. Thus possible opposition is intimidated by propaganda, which precisely brands those who do not cooperate with the political project as ungrateful. At the same time, mayors are careful not to declare that they are no longer able (if ever they were) to keep their election promises.

Role-playing presupposes a dependence of social integration on shared values, according to a character already given in advance, a script already written, or a scene already set up, where participants try to do their best with the roles that have been arranged in advance. This explains why role-playing games have helped in training classrooms to express that dualism between subjectivity and society characteristic of so many areas of psychological and social theory. The problem is not only of a theoretical dualism but also of a disorientation of everyday acting, where people no longer know which parts to take: the reassuring script of the time, if it ever existed, is certainly no longer there today (Ritzer, 2007). It becomes increasingly difficult today to get it right as a parent, mayor, doctor, leader, or mediator of a community. The role is no longer internalized by the subject from a cultural repertoire as the setting of role playing leads one to think, but is formed in face-to-face interaction with other subjects, in an uninterrupted process of approximations by trial and error. The emergence of sociological games lies in the need to stage this profound transformation of social interactions and study its ongoing causes and effects.

Social positioning behaviors are constructed during games, each time, in unique and unrepeatable ways, but also following regularities, which show how the production of subjectivity and structures is possible in contemporary society. Subjectivities and social structures are constructed as intersections of discourses, relations, and legitimations, emerging from the typing processes of the participants. For example, those who play mayor or doctor interpret their roles according to ways of thinking typical of common sense and at the same time intertwined with what is happening in the course of the game, starting from the interaction with the other participants, who in turn, acting in the same way, contribute to the definition of the situation, its constraints, and structural possibilities. A social positioning involves the creation of a type-ideal defined within a web of mutual, unique, and unrepeatable relationships, and from a particular repertoire of norms and sanctions referring to the regional culture of the local group.

The sociological game, although it carries with it a number of structural constraints (specified in a very vague way, as we shall see in the presentation of individual games) is characterized by such a wide field of choice, signification, and legitimation that it is up to the participant to exercise or absolve the prerogatives of his position, according to his own style, regional culture, and the conditions of co-presence between actors. Positioning in the spatio-temporal path of the sociological game is for each participant the reproduction of a life cycle. The formation of a social position is recursively based on a mimetic phase of mirroring, where the participant learns to reflect on what he is doing and on the effects of his choices, through the image that others return to him with respect to his body, that is, the plasticity of his presence and his conduct. The very connotation of a specific social position necessarily depends on a certain serial repetition of action and discourse. Of course, positioning also depends on the processes of categorization and social differentiation. Being a mayor, a clan leader, or a Spartan champion is different by physiological (it still takes *phisique du rôle*!), historical, and cultural criteria. But it is the intersection of locally emerging specific dynamics, on the one hand, and long-lasting historical processes, on the other, that creates the overall picture of the social positioning process. Only within the framework of such interconnection, within broader institutionalized structures, is it possible to interpret the spatiotemporal co-presence of uniqueness and regularity in relation to the duality of subject and society (Elias, 1977).

Role-playing, as presupposed by the dramaturgical framework of the term (as well as the ambivalence of playing, which implies both playing and acting), is effective in contexts of social interaction, in which rights and duties, tasks and deliveries, and cultures and rituals can be formulated with relative clarity. The limitations of its application in educational and training contexts, as many critics of its freewheeling use have noted, are largely due to the fact that today, in social, organizational, and community contexts, it is increasingly difficult to identify a consensus on precisely those rights and duties, those tasks and deliveries, and those cultures and rituals—in a word, on the meaning of those supposed values (Berger & Luckmann, 1995). The problem is perhaps just the opposite, namely, to identify the appropriate methods for reaching a shareable value vision, not to take the terms of the convention for granted but to negotiate ways to approach sharing them.

Positioning touches the heart of the matter because it refers to the contextuality of social relations. It can be seen as the unique yet regular occurrence of interactions that build and dissolve, quickly and unstably, in focused spatial-temporal arcs. The process of consolidation of social position occurs primarily by repetition. The repetitive, not to say ritualistic, nature of most courses of strategic action is what makes the behavior stable, but it requires participants to invest increasing energy and constantly maintain their level of participation. The protagonists of the games often transform some implicit values of the exercise into social positionings, e.g., "I am a good mayor," "I am a charismatic leader," "I am a skilled negotiator." Validation of this individual hypothesis about one's own interaction style comes only from the other participants, in a repetition of reciprocal relays and mirroring. Validation may come through messages with the most varied forms of expression, words, nods, glances, smiles, or blushes, etc. In this way, some people come across as more authoritative, more seductive, or more sociable than others, but in reality this depends, in a way that games make increasingly explicit, on the skills of controlling and managing two kinds of information: that which we detect from others and that which others receive from us. In an individualistic and competitive society, such as the contemporary one (Tomelleri, 2009), sociological games help participants orient themselves to how social placements work.

When humans play games they are already defined in their identity or, if you prefer, in the repertoire of their social positionings because of the contexts they frequent on a daily basis. Sociological games allow them to question their identity through an ongoing exploration of possibilities for action, staying within more permeable boundaries and being able to experiment with backtracking to avoid otherwise negative relational consequences. These games are activities that constitute unique and unrepeatable worlds, a matrix of possible events and a complex of placements, which when they occur create a world of their own, different from other worlds (Riezler, 1941). It often happened during experiments with sociological games that a unique set of meanings, idioms, and behaviors was produced that depended on the players' interaction activities, isolating them from the outside world and absorbing them entirely. Nonetheless, this referred not so much to the surreptitious assumption of a predetermined social role but to the dynamics of the game itself, such that by playing one tends to reproduce in a simulated context—in some ways protected, but for that very reason all the more exposed to the weather of relationships—the social bond constitutive of the group (Boockok & Coleman, 1966).

In order to play, people must agree not so much on individual rules, but that the rules must be obeyed, assuming the risk that someone may cheat even on that agreement. While playing the game, no merely utilitarian exchange or action is possible without a more or less implicit agreement, precisely, or without there having previously been a sharing of the rules to be observed. Play implies a pre-contractual solidarity underlying all group action, which in social terms we have called, in previous chapters, the sympathy between the people involved. The pre-contractual in play corresponds to the pre-contractual in the construction of the perceptual image; in both cases, it is not a matter of positive negotiation over specific content, but rather of the enactment of collective involvement. As Wittgenstein would put it, it is the "mystical" game of morality, whereby it is not this or that rule that needs to be discussed, but that there are rules (Wittgenstein, 1922/1969, § 6.44: "Not *how* the world is, is the mystical, but *that* it is"; see on this also Hadot, 2005).

However, and here we come to the risk alluded to earlier, one should not confuse this analytical primacy of sympathy with the empirical situation, where from time to time solidarity on the basis of shared values may be fluctuating and temporary. What gives rise to this solidarity? What is the social foundation, we might say, of the feeling of trust? We cannot assume that there is always—sometimes people choose not to play—but we can certainly be able to predict which will be the included or excluded of trust: sometimes in fact some people are obliged not to play. The mechanisms of social exclusion are not the outcome of a failed negotiation but are part and parcel of the original distinction that makes the game emerge. That distinction takes the form of a decision about the game itself: "Let's play!" already means "Let's trust each other that we are playing!" which sometimes also implies "I don't trust you!" All this means that there are no normative structures external to the game that can guarantee its functioning; the pre-contractual dimension of the decision about the game is not a technological accessory but an internal condition. The dynamic that produces solidarity, that is, the social bond based on trust, is the repetition of the interaction or, in other words, the game itself.

4.2. Open Sesame!

Once decided, play opens up a world and immediately closes it in on itself. The decision about the game implies the transition to a society in a simulated environment, which reproduces and amplifies the social relations internalized through individual cultural traditions of belonging, or even the learning styles that are activated in the process of play itself. For these reasons, we have identified a kind of evolutionary path of the games we propose in this text. However, by "evolution," we do not mean a teleology, either in a positive sense (the tendency toward progress) or in a negative sense (the tendency toward decadence or degeneration). Evolution means, in this case, the awareness of different levels of social complexity coming into play, literally, in the scenarios. Therefore, we move from the primitive, tribal social situation

(Tribes) to the archaic war duel (Thermopylae) to the institutionalization of socio-cultural issues (Polis) to the extreme tensions of the post-human (Collapse) and apocalyptic (Zombies) contexts.

If we have chosen these scenarios and this somewhat historical succession of playful proposals, it is therefore not to endorse a positivistic view of society and the human behaviors and values that take place in it; on the contrary, we like to think that social structure as such is characterized by a "viscous" consistency, as Sartre (1947) would say, that is, an intermediate stage between the solid and the liquid, between plastic and quantifiable concreteness and the disturbing elusiveness of continuous change (Bauman, 2000). The image of the viscous structure is even more pregnant, in its non-teleological valence, if we talk about games: There are, in fact, no games that are "better" or "worse" than others. The judgment of progression or regression on a game, typical of psychodynamic observation, does not belong to the sociological register. As with art, one cannot abandon positive teleology (*à la* Vasari) for a negative teleology that laments the ineluctable degeneration of taste (Didi-Huberman, 1998).

The thin historical line that accompanies sociological games is actually a narrative artifice, an expository convenience, rather than a structural element. The story we seek to tell is a problematic one, that is, it is based on the particular problems we intend to subject to the dynamics of the game. We begin with Tribe, in which we highlight the emergence of leadership beyond the crisis that the principle of authority (or, as Jacques Lacan would say, the "master's discourse") has been suffering in recent decades. This game sets up the basic social conditions for understanding what it means to choose a leader in a group and what skills are needed to tolerate its subsistence or to question its power.

The second play, Thermopylae, makes explicit the conflict dynamics inherent in any social group. If we accept the phenomenological-existential hypothesis that play is an integral part of the human experience (Fink, 1968), or even take into account the socio-historical theories that make play an irreducible and crucial reality of culture (Huizinga, 1938/2002; Caillois, 1958), we are equally driven to grasp the violent matrix manifested in play, both on the ethological level of learning to fight and on the strategic-military level of electing and annihilating the enemy. Playing, in short, in some ways means from the outset playing against someone. In this sense, the choice of the Greco-Persian setting seemed fitting, in its extreme coercion to binary deployment, where otherness is immediately configured as hostile, with no possibility of predetermined elaboration other than the contingent outcome of a "move" of the game.

The third scenario we propose is the most tested and the closest, perhaps, to contemporary educational experience. Polis is a game that intends to revisit the place that quintessentially constitutes the fulcrum of social life: polis, the square, which in recent years is particularly suffering from a process of inexorable annihilation. However, still today most institutions move and interact in a series of simulated squares, in an incidental atmosphere, as if poleis still existed, as if the democratic process of representation and negotiation still played an indispensable role. That is why it seems to us appropriate to reflect on these practices, relearning the ancient gestures of diplomacy and compromise, of assertiveness and public participation, to the extent that these gestures find themselves mimicked and mortified by the abstract practices of today's politics and organizations.

After the experience of participating in public activity, we address the extreme crisis with Collapse; a game with an apocalyptic setting, Collapse owes much to science fiction literature but also to the eco-eschatological reflections of Jared Diamond (2005) and sociological reflection on the crisis of human nature (Fuller, 2006; Sloterdijk, 2006) and the dynamics of victimhood as a social precipitate of contemporary history (Tomelleri, 2009). This game pushes participants to confront the possibility of rebuilding a lost bond, using unusual means and knowledge, discovering potentialities and skills long since dormant or repressed by the constraints and coercions of dominant hyper-consumption and technology.

Finally, in a context that further deepens the apocalyptic scenario, we bring into play the very figure of the end of the world: the zombie. Zombies is a sociological game that allows us to visualize not only the fundamental emotions of social life, beginning with fear, but also the equally fundamental strategies that in a more or less automatic way are enacted to cope with affective arousal, especially violence.

These five games suggest the possibility of formulating a kind of ludic synthesis of contemporary society as a response to the crisis of meaning that—far from affecting so-called everyday life, or bothering the so-called man in the street—imposes itself as a nihilistic verb; moralistic rhetoric; and political alibi for manipulating the minds, bodies, wallets, and lives of today's men and women. Beyond the crisis of meaning and inner turmoil, sociological games propose a practical way for a fruitful testing of human capacities. They are a suggestion for a new way of doing social science, of doing education, and of getting involved in the constitutive practices of being human.

CHAPTER 5

Tribe

The Leader and the Sacrifice

TRIBE IS A SOCIOLOGICAL COMMUNITY WORKSHOP, AIMED AT THOSE who work, at various levels of responsibility, in social and complex organizations. It is an individual, group, and community laboratory, which, in its evolution, increases personal reflexivity on transversal skills (negotiating, mediating, diagnosing critical relational issues, problem-solving, etc.) and social skills (analyzing institutionalization processes, defining social parts and scripts, reading of cultural contexts, and producing structures of power) and on leadership styles (authoritarian, democratic, participatory, cooperative, etc.). Tribe is thus a relational context that develops participants' attention to the social processes of leadership construction, highlighting the emotional scope of these processes and the (often overlooked) link between affectivity and institutional organization (e.g., the desire for recognition, or the nexus between fear and authority).

The methodology of the game is participatory; it triggers an interactive dynamic, which tends to be competitive and conflictual, requiring participants to make continuous personal adjustments and repositionings in relation to the production of events, symbols, and meanings. Specifically, it involves experimenting with how much it "costs" (in personal, group, and social terms) to be a leader or to be a "wingman," and how much each of the participants is willing to lose, sacrifice, or invest for a cause they believe is just. Often, in ordinary group dynamics, these elements remain implicit, fueling an undercurrent of envy, a sense of inadequacy, and resentment, which, in turn, consolidates the general malaise of a team, a class, or an office.

Tribe, of course, like all simulations, is by no means a panacea. It is not meant to "solve" problems once and for all, but to make them recognizable and palpable, and thus to allow participants to think about problems reflexively—in their concreteness—in a protected context. This is important, because unreflected dynamics, in fact, objectify and reify themselves into as many mute symbols, "totems" of the absolute distance of a problem from its possible solution. In its tested version, Tribe requires between sixteen participants and thirty participants. The workshop involves the activation of a process of electing a leader within a group. The gradual and progressive institutionalization of its actions and decisions interacts with the activity of the group, which in a succession of stages is faced with complex tasks.

5.1. The Original Scene

Tribe draws suggestions and sap from Sigmund Freud's *Totem and Taboo*, a book that has marked, as few others, the cultural destiny not only of psychoanalysis but also of the way of considering the deep history of human nature (Tomelleri & Doni, 2009). The totem is, generally speaking, the figure with which a collectivity is identified: in the Australian societies studied by early modern and contemporary social scientists, the totem takes on an explicit normative significance, embodying a living creature that represents an ancestor of the clan that identifies with it. As a primary law, the totem takes under its protection those who claim to be its "children" and who therefore accept the prohibition against eating the meat of the totem animal. Regardless of the ethnographic correctness of these considerations, which over the past century have often been questioned, the idea of the totem plays an interesting orienting role in understanding the functioning of a group. Therefore, it is inevitable to juxtapose the totem to a tribe, in which the totem recognizes and confirms itself. The convenience of using this "archaic" instrumentation is twofold: On the one hand, it shifts the participants' attention to a fantastical narrative plane, unrelated to the opaque everyday life they experience, thus allowing them to observe their own behaviors without being sidetracked by engaging and compromising considerations. On the other hand, it touches the deep chords, if one can say so, of the human soul, those that insist on the readiness for conflict or surrender, allowing the participants to highlight their emotional and cognitive resilience within a path of development and innovation.

5.2. The Unexpected and the Crisis

Tribe highlights, among the members of a community, the confrontation with the genesis of the figure of the leader. It is obvious that in today's institutional contexts this confrontation with the emergent process of leadership never occurs so explicitly and directly; less obvious is the fact that, precisely because of the series of bureaucratic or ritual mediations we put in place to loosen our grip on authority, we tend all the more to construct imaginary alternative figures to the "body" of the leader. The series of medial procedures that stand between a subject and the decision-maker figure form the backbone of a society's wheels, and their removal is, in some ways, a violation of laws and norms of behavior. When we skip a step in a procedure, we are usually sanctioned, while we observe with indignation, mixed with envy, the lucky ones who have connections with the "higher-ups," who in no time manage to get away with it. All this has to do with the difficulty with which we now, in the generally democratic system in which we live and in which we grew up, recognize authority. Unlike in archaic societies, in which power is acquired in accordance with cosmic or divine forces that distribute and sanction it, in democratic societies power is diffuse (this is the literal meaning of "democracy"): That is, it is less visible. It is intangible, and, when it is exercised within a group, it must be justified. This means that while a leader in an archaic society does not have to mince words, because his is the only word that counts, within today's group the identification of the leader takes an extra strain in terms of availability, tightness, and assurance, etc. And what is worse, all this remains more often than not in the background of relationships.

A sociologically and historically important strategy to overcome these difficulties has been, for many centuries, the institutionalization of hierarchy. The construction of stratified social relations has resulted in a kind of organized compartmentalization in some institutions, such that the discourse of those who occupy the upper part was assumed as the norm by the lower part. Formally, most institutions today still function this way. However, the rapid transformation of the foundations on which the liberal culture of the West rests, to which we lately give the name of "crisis"—but which is not only about the economic and financial crisis—has exposed in a sometimes violent way the flaws that have opened in this hierarchical structure (Tomelleri, 2009).

Two examples suffice as a guiding parameter. The corporatization of the health service has meant that the general practitioner, what in Italy—a hundred years ago—used to be called the *medico condotto*—the conducted doctor (i.e., called by the mayor of the village or, as was often the case, by the parish priest)—has been transformed into a kind of catchment area. The social outcome of this transformation has been that we no longer witness, or we witness less and less, the scene of the doctor who, after his shift in the clinic is over, goes around the village to visit the elderly lady, the child, the pregnant woman, etc. Instead, we witness quite different scenes: overflowing waiting rooms, packed agendas, telephone reservations, and bagged prescriptions without a visit worthy of the name. The political virtue of the doctor, the one that made the doctor a social authority recognized by a group, has evaporated within a few decades, in favor of a bureaucratic functionality that has faded in no small measure the aura of power attached to the caring relationship. This tendency is made even more dramatically evident in educational relationships: the teacher of yesteryear is no longer the unquestioned authority of the class group; he no longer has anything to do with the paternalistic affectation of a De Amicis. He is more akin to a cultural mediator, whose eventual awkwardnesses are punctually and ruthlessly filmed by the most astute pupils, who broadcast the performances of what, until not so long ago, was the main point of reference for secondary socialization on the internet.

From our point of view, it is neither a matter here of proposing a nostalgic attitude, as if to say that "it was better before," nor of tracing an apocalyptic panorama, which is a very easy and inexpensive thing to do, but ultimately useless and indeed potentially pathogenic for social relations. What is important is to observe, in this general picture, the detachment of the leader from his visible legitimacy, from his recognition, and thus the bewilderment into which professional figures involved in leadership relations sometimes run. There is no longer, therefore, a "substantive" reason for ascribing authority: The "etiquette," on which the court society was founded, the one—to be clear—that between the seventeenth and eighteenth centuries "invented" the modern hierarchy, is completely thrown off balance. The classical references are at a deadweight loss. It is therefore necessary to face the emotional scope of this epochal threshold and to elaborate appropriate cognitive strategies to maintain a constructive social balance.

5.3. Game Preparation

The preparation of the game takes about thirty minutes. At this stage, it is first necessary to set up the context and describe the main rules of the game. Tribe requires a minimum number of sixteen participants and an appropriate space with movable chairs. The use of flip charts and ordinary stationery is recommended (but not essential). The presenters will have cards with them with the "talents" discussed in Phase 2 (see below). The team of trainers consists of two or three people; the presence of the third trainer depends on the degree of analysis and detail of the observations. After the presentation of the team of trainers to the assembly of participants, a presenter introduces the purpose of the workshop, the methodology, and the entire workshop program. Tribe includes a first part of exercises and a second part of shared reflections in the groups and assembly. The workshop is described in all its phases, specifying the deliverables. Participants may ask for clarifications or further details. Once the exercise has begun, participants should carry out one phase at a time, without anticipating the deliverables planned in subsequent phases.

At this point, we begin with the description of the historical and social scenario: about five thousand years ago, a tribe of hunter-gatherers, located in a specific space (which it will be up to the imagination of the participants to enrich with details) must choose its leader who will have to carry out one of the proposals of the clans that compose the tribe.

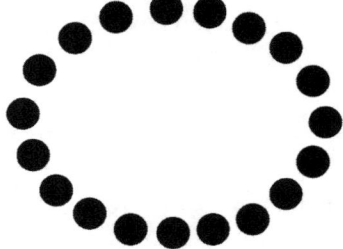 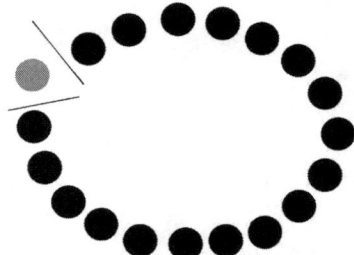

FIGURE 1. The circular arrangement of Tribe participants.

FIGURE 2. Tribe leader withdraws from the group.

5.4. Conduct

1. First group meeting (forty-five minutes). The group is arranged in a circle, according to the arrangement in figure 1. The group meets to carry out the first delivery. Participants must choose one leader within the group for the entire duration of the exercise. There is no particular instruction that should condition the choice of leader.
2. Second meeting of the group. Part 1 (forty-five minutes). The leader withdraws from the group as shown in figure 2. From this point on, he/she will be responsible for the progress of the exercise and adherence to the work steps.

    Each group member is randomly given one or more "gifts" or virtues (given in the following list) by the leader. Only the leader knows all the available endowments, while the group members know only those that have fallen to them by chance. It is necessary for the distribution of the endowments to take place randomly and individually, because within the group only the leader should know the actual potential of the collective. Once the distribution has taken place, the following question is asked, "What are you willing to donate to the community, and what instead would you prefer to keep for yourself, among the objects and symbols that have randomly been handed to you, as an inheritance, for the realization of the final choice?" The nature of the final choice is not made explicit,

List of Endowments to Be Distributed Randomly

tent	clay	arrows	bricks
magic	children	cymbals	honey
pots	shield	seeds	poison
fire	writing	hammer	masks
hatchet	spear	friendly tribes	ropes
salt	dagger	game	women
wheel	numbers	sickle	latrines
ropes	ornaments	unknown lands	opium
water	bows	traps	copper
bison skin	drums	magic	frame
clothing	medicinal herbs	dogs	constellations

but it is anticipated that it is a momentous decision regarding the very development and survival of the group. The leader is excluded from this commitment, because he receives no endowment, but decides whether donations are sufficient and appropriate. He cannot force anyone to donate, but he can refuse to accept donations as a whole. If the leader deems the donation insufficient, the exercise should be repeated until the donations reach an adjusted quantitative and qualitative quota.

3. The final decision (thirty minutes). The leader gathers the clan representatives and chooses which project to carry out, after hearing the representatives and discussing with them the design criteria, how to work as a group and the purpose of the project. Only spokespersons may speak at this stage (see figure 4). Other participants are not allowed to intervene in the discussion, otherwise the clan will be excluded from the negotiation table. The leader is placed in the center and has the spokespersons in front of him, who in turn precede the other clan members arranged in a radial pattern. The chief is responsible for managing the conversation, encouraging dialogue, listening to each other, and respecting turns to speak. Should the chief favor a clan project, it will be necessary to negotiate the eventuality of one or more endowments that, strategically or accidentally, have appeared in the negotiation: the new endowments,

in fact, are the property of the clan, which may decide not to share them with other clans that do not approve of its decisions. This phase will end when time runs out or when the leader has chosen which project to implement.
4. The showdown (twenty minutes). You return to the starting position (figure 1). Each member of the tribe is asked to declare whether or not he or she agrees with the project espoused by the leader. This is an intermediate stage between the conclusion of the game and its reworking. The presenters do not intervene except to manage turns to speak.
5. Feedback (thirty minutes). At this point the game is over. The presenters take the floor and reconstruct the tribe's story. Depending on the style of conducting and the conformation of the group, restitution can be set on the channels of social emotionality (asking participants key questions, e.g., "How did you feel?," "What did you feel?," etc.) or on that of building the hierarchical network of conflict and/or collaboration. The purpose of restitution should not be to validate the decision made by the leader but to clarify the dynamics that that decision generated within the group. Participants are thus called to an exercise in mirroring their own social practices. There is, in fact, no "right" Tribe solution. There are, however, endless possibilities for understanding one's actions within the environment in which one lives, works, or studies.

5.5. From Fear of Authority to Sacrifice

The Tribe experience is unique, and theoretical reflection is generated in the face-to-face interaction among participants and between the presenters and participants. Each time, the specificity of the target territory, organizational contexts, and participants' professional histories, as well as the unique dynamic evolution of the exercise, cause different themes to emerge. Although in distinct ways, some guiding themes nevertheless tend to emerge recurrently. Below, as in the notes to the other sociological games that will follow, we recall briefly, and without claiming to be exhaustive, some of the guiding themes that in the course of the different experiments we have had the opportunity to discuss and explore with the various participants. Some

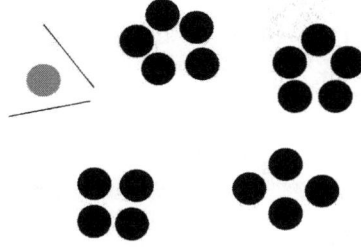

FIGURE 3. Clans work out their plan, and chief observes.

of what we have elaborated would never have seen the light of day without them; for this and for the pleasant formative days spent together, we are very grateful to them.

Between Equality and Hierarchy

Tribe from the very beginning of its unfolding poses a number of critical issues that arise from the ineradicable relationship between formal social equality and more or less explicit de facto power hierarchies within any social context. Especially in the first stage of the exercise, when the leader is to be elected, relations are spread that are simultaneously competitive (caused by the fact that anyone can be the chosen one) and unequal (caused by the multiplicity of choice variables at play: skills, desires, values, ideas, alliances, friendships, etc.). Inequality among group members becomes more pronounced in the second stage, when endowments are randomly distributed, and the actual possession of assets can establish new power hierarchies, in addition to the great power difference between the leader and the group. Within this framework, more and more members of the tribe feel uncertain about their ability to evaluate the actions to be taken and to predict the outcomes of the workshop. All this poses the problem, especially for the chief, of preventing paralysis from excesses of indecision. In fact, one of the risks that each actor in the workshop experiences is that distrust, when it prevails over possible evolutionary developments in interactions, leads to paralysis of action.

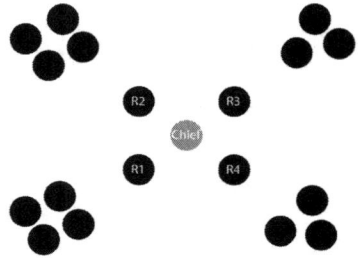

FIGURE 4. The chief and representatives.

Emotions and Social Structuring

Tribe offers participants the opportunity to grasp the poignancy of the relationship between emotions and the process of structuring a social order. This relationship is at first uncertain and indeterminate. Indeed, the absence of a common power makes it difficult to determine what is right or what is not. And without a common power, participants are hardly able to judge in their emotions. It is in this way that the actors discover that their own organization is not a distinct and separate reality from the relationships they weave among themselves and the emotional and affective phenomena these entail. The relationship between organization and group structure, on the one hand, and emotional and affective experiences, on the other, is by no means obvious, nor is it a matter of easy reflection to handle. On the contrary, it is very often on this ridge that conflicts, misunderstandings, and frictions are played out, seemingly trivial but which, if not worked out, risk festering to the point of mutual intolerance.

Fear of Authority

Working groups, placed in the "elementary" conditions of social life, highlight the primary dynamics of relationships, particularly the uneasy relationship with authority. Uneasy, because authority, real power and its management, are relational dimensions generated in conflict, on the basis of physical and/or charismatic superiority that is never guaranteed once and for all, nor is it itself necessarily a guarantor of stability and consistency. Authority is sometimes respected formally but belied in marginal social contexts, where more or less explicit resistance is identified. In Tribe, different scenarios can open up: the "weak" can manifest their awe of the "strong" in many ways, while the latter tend to express anxiety about the preservation of their hegemony, becoming in this way social "reactionaries"; alternatively, the marginalized have the opportunity to organize formulas of innovation that the "strong," by virtue of the preservation of hegemony, can neither foresee nor oppose.

Social Effervescence and Control

According to Emile Durkheim (1912), the state of effervescence characterizes social groups that experience "dynamic density," that is contexts in which many people experience the same emotional tensions. The social action experienced in Tribe involves the experience of crisis. Crisis situations, in any group, deal with the most ambivalent emotional dimensions: flight and avoidance, on the one hand, recklessness and interventionism, on the other. In this sense, crisis disposes group members in a ritual condition of "dynamic density," or effervescence, in which the normative frames of ritual (of "manners," hierarchical ordering, etc.; Elias, 1933/1983) are perceived as fragile and porous. The same effervescence, while caught in moments of exaltation or panic, is also regarded with awe, especially by those in leadership positions, whether or not such positions are effective in the work context. One way of observing social dynamics is possible if we consider the processes of control of effervescence and the pockets of containment that are identified throughout the various sequences of play.

Styles of Action between Uncertainty and Routine

Every social action involves the elaboration of a ritual, more or less rigidly institutionalized. The margins of freedom granted within rituals are what we call "style." The style of action is identifiable in its oscillations between two extremes: sharp and aggressive violation of ritual norms (quarrel, insubordination, abandonment of the setting, etc.) and complete standardization of behavior (avoidance, uncritical reproduction of norms foreign to the setting). Uncertainty and routine make it possible, when considered as behavioral polarities, to also identify styles of action based on elementary variables, such as that of gender, age, work seniority, etc. In this sense, it is appropriate to reread the experiences brought into play starting from the style polarization and then arriving at the elemental variables, in order to avoid reducing social complexities to stereotypes already acted out by the dominant group or cultures.

Leadership Styles

Leadership style can take many forms. It can be rational, charismatic, traditionalist, instrumental, collaborative, or alienating, etc. Here we focus on some recurring dynamics: Laxity occurs when the leader becomes disinterested in the tribe's activities, stands aside, lets decisions be made without directly intervening. Participation, on the other hand, occurs when the leader tries to involve everyone in the group's discussion and decision-making, expressing his feelings and opinions without judging or evaluating other members of the tribe, welcoming with a constructive attitude the criticisms that others make to him, and attempting, whenever possible, to use conflicts as a way to promote a positive confrontation of ideas. Conversely, directiveness occurs when one tries to impose his will or values on other members of the group, e.g., when he is not able to intervene in the group's activities, when the leader uses means of coercion to get others to support his decisions anyway, when he makes evaluations or judgments about tribe members, blocking the action of a clan or tribe member, or when he forces the group to make a decision or organize itself. Finally, there is do-goodism, when his attitude is to avoid conflict or unpleasant feelings by "pouring oil on troubled waters," or when he speaks only to compliment others (Ciulla, 2020).

Styles of Influence

Tribe's social actors learn that every interpersonal relationship is governed by certain fundamental structures, such as modes of relationship or styles of relating, which influence the people interacting in various ways. The process of influencing, in its relational qualities, shows itself most clearly when the actors in the relationship are making a decision and therefore have to confront each other about possible choices. Influencing styles can refer to different discursive registers of the moralistic type, such as moral pressure (judging others' behaviors, prescribing goals, offering incentives, exerting blackmail, etc.), the do-gooder type (recognizing and involving others, expressing understanding), the collectivist type (building a common vision, identifying opportunities, defining a common path), and the rational-utilitarian type (standardizing procedures, manipulating, convincing).

Scapegoating

The actors in Tribe experience that every social order is capable of generating scapegoats within itself, feeding antagonistic and destructive tensions (Girard, 1982; Dumouchel, 2015). Hence the reflexive awareness that there exists in every human group someone who more or less unconsciously draws upon himself and around him the internal discontents of the group. The vivid emergence of a leader generates at its opposite the opaque concealment of a scapegoat, who becomes the designated victim of the antagonistic dynamics internal to the social order of Tribe. The tribe's scapegoat, the excluded, the one who is marginalized, may turn out to be the leader who is progressively removed from the group and placed on the margins of interaction processes.

The presenters will always have to ask themselves where and how the danger is hidden—inherent in the very dynamics of the workshop—of triggering processes of excluding the leader, a clan, or an individual participant. In this way, exclusion becomes a privileged vantage point for understanding the logics of power reproduction in that specific social context. The process of marginalization becomes a general tool of inquiry, enabling presenters to grasp the forms and processes of social dynamics and at the same time to contribute to the construction of a culture of social relations that is, as far as possible, nonviolent.

Altruism

The workshop offers actors the opportunity to recognize the value of cooperative interaction and solidarity. Self-centered and individualistic behaviors and discourses, although they continue to be considered the main reference with which we talk about ourselves and "serious" things (economics, politics, etc.), in Tribe show all their limitations. As the exercise evolves, we learn that mistrust, selfishness, and individual self-interest lead to paralysis and frustration, while altruism, which is not petty charity but the concrete recognition of the other person and his or her "gifts," allows the most difficult situations to be unblocked. Cooperative interaction turns out to be the anthropological and sociological condition that enables collective enterprise.

The Exact Imagination

The telling and prefiguring of possible scenarios plays a crucial function in the evolutionary or involutional development of Tribe. The setting of the exercise's "prehistoric" scenario prompts participants to construct contexts and formulate hypotheses far removed from their everyday lives, but nonetheless relevant to their own existential and professional path. For this reason, the narrative mode is not simply a frill or a decorative addition: rather, it is the fundamental medium by which the social meanings of the group are conveyed.

CHAPTER 6

Thermopylae

Playing at War

THE THERMOPYLAE IS A GAME OF A VERY PARTICULAR TYPE, WHICH we might call a socio-historical game. It is a multiple-step exercise, which aims to increase evaluation skills in a regulated competition. It is aimed at all those who, in various capacities (operators, planners, coordinators, managers, administrators), work in professional situations where the collaborative network is characterized by a strong sense of competition. One of the fundamental intents of this game, in fact, is to show the facets of competitive practices, which are often highly emotionally charged conflict dimensions but not as well recognized, let alone rationalized (Tomelleri, 2009).

Thermopylae is a group and inter-group game that stimulates imagination to foster reflexivity about the processes and dynamics of the violent drift that is always possible in social relations. The game reproduces an ambivalent scenario of antagonism where conflict can degenerate into the violence of war. The event of war makes present the eventuality of defeat, which in common sense is systematically removed at the hands of a widespread culture of efficient performance. Defeat is when men realize that they will no longer die one at a time, but in large numbers, gaining awareness of the possible systematic destruction of their community. But those who wage war are not only afraid of defeat, they also have the excitement, as monstrous as it is fascinating, of being able to win over the enemy.

The possibility of crushing the adversary is a form of "enjoyment of evil," which responds to a structural truth of the human being, whereby the seduction for one's own and others' destruction exists in each person (Lacan, 1975). Play reproduces the ambivalence of what Freud called the "death drive" (Freud, 1920/1955), a drive toward evil and one's own destruction, which the playful dimension makes recognizable and conscious. Without looking for the scapegoat or feeding a moralistic judgment on human behavior, the play downplays the obscene fascination with war and measures itself against some anthropological and sociological determinants of human nature. More specifically, Thermopylae is a game that activates in participants the evaluation and analysis of some specific areas of the ambivalence of social action in conflict contexts:

- One area is the distinction between subjective and objective meaning of a social action, whereby the subjective meaning of the action remains mostly inaccessible to objective understanding; that is, there is an unbridgeable gap between the subjective intention and the dynamic effects of the action: for example, when a person wishes to make a gesture of affection (giving a gift or preparing a romantic dinner, etc.) but the gesture is inappropriate by excess or default (the gift or dinner is not liked).
- Another is the distinction between onstage and offstage, whereby there are circumstances where individuals act according to formalized roles and offstage spaces where individuals set the stage furniture to prepare for direct confrontation; for example, when an operator prepares an educational or social integration intervention and must necessarily distinguish between what is permissible to say to the audience and what must not be said to ensure the successful outcome of the action.
- Another is the distinction between "public" and "private" in behavior, whereby social action acquires irreducible meaning when it is carried out within a group, rather than when it is carried out in solitude (if it is ever possible to speak of social action in solitude); the rituals of interaction, which govern social encounters (rules of conversation, patterns of behavior, use of conventional signals), and their essential function in the construction of a group's identity.

- Another is the way in which "successes" and "defeats" are processed, prompting analysis of the cultures that move to promote one or avert the other.

The methodology of the game is fully infomed and participatory, i.e., those who play know from the outset everything they need to be able to choose their moves. They are thus empowered to construct their own experience. Such a methodology triggers a competitive dynamic that promotes the analysis and change of personal styles of social interaction, promotes personal evaluation of the constraints and possibilities given by a specific context with all its ambivalences, urges the unmasking of strategies of manipulation and continuous adjustments for the production of information, and seeks to answer the formative questions (of meaning, analysis, and evaluation) that emerge from the crisis of social organizations.

Thermopylae requires a minimum number of twelve participants and a maximum of twenty-one. The game involves a succession of complex phases and different levels of strategic interaction. For optimal conduct of the game, a full day should be spent on it. The game, after all, can be considered a kind of crash course in decision-making action. What is important, however, is that it is a game, that is, a practice that activates social actions. Like all games, it is therefore not so much about theoretical content or technical notions as it is about experiences. In this case, it is about a process in which three groups (Athenians, Spartans, and Persians) characterized by a specific ambivalent reference context—which will force them to choose mainly between two options, war or peace—interact with each other. Actions and coalitions follow one another according to a different script each time that the groups elaborate, changing the horizon and perspectives. Each move of the game, therefore, is a way for participants to make themselves increasingly protagonists of a story, or if you will, of a "counter-story," which in turn, as we shall see, reveals the ability to construct strategic interactions in organizational realities. The course of the game is punctuated by a regulated series of group meetings, alternating with moments of inter-group meetings, called the arena (figure 5). The term arena comes from the Latin *areo*, which refers to that which is dry and arid. The earliest form is *asena*, and so it may also refer to the Sanskrit root as, "to lie," that is, "the thing that lies, that

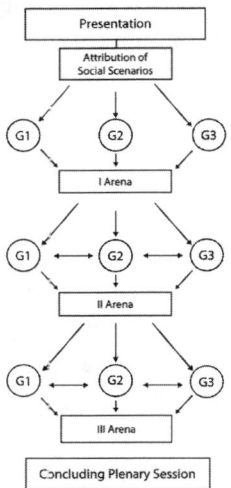

FIGURE 5. Thermopylae.

lies at the bottom of the sea." The arena represents the driest part of the earth, devoid of fruitful humus: it is the desert. Figuratively speaking, it is the space in the middle of an amphitheater and circus, so called because of the sand with which it was strewn. The choice to refer to the arena hints at the regulated game of conflict and the deeply barren and disruptive nature of all warfare.

6.1. Why Play War?

The Battle of Thermopylae (480 BC) is perhaps the mother of all battles; the imagination, which is the very lifeblood of games and in general, we believe, of social life, is inevitably stimulated by such a stark, limpid, obvious scenario: two opposing fronts, two absolute powers, two conflicting epics, two models of heroism, that is, of humanity, compared. Real life, of course, is not like that (Cartledge, 2006), and the game of Thermopylae is perhaps the appropriate play to realize this; however, every beginning needs an archetypal image, so to speak. And the image of the battlefront is perhaps the best rendering of what is at stake.

Holding this image still, let us try to ask why on earth, in a training context, such a scene should be set up. The point is this: Imagery is not, on closer inspection, a matter of individual free will. Creativity does not work on command. The battle scene is a constant presence in the metaphors that are used to define roles, competencies, priorities, and decisions. Images are not simply figures of speech but are cognitive styles that in turn underlie determined social practices. The link between these practices and the images that conveyed them is almost always unconscious. However, this link lingers, and to ignore it is also to ignore the potentially destructive scope of the conflict dynamics that are lodged in every relationship.

In addition, it should be considered that the opportunity to revive the subject's awe of the vital interweavings between self and historical context (which, among other things, allows one to grasp the cultural significance of the social sciences) arises from the realization that daily problems, even when they refer to issues beyond the individual's scope of action, tend to be traced back to the "dark forces" within him anyway. The search for the causes of malaise within man, and not in his relation to society and history, denies the opportunity to imagine vital interdependencies, outside ordinary patterns. This is the profound reason for Thermopylae, its emergence, if one may say so, from the historical and social consistency of human nature, and thus not from intrapsychic conflicts and solipsistic reductionisms. Thermopylae reproduces this ineradicable tension between individual courses of action and the surrounding space, showing the link that exists between the constraints and resources of a given historical scenario and the capacity of social actors to imagine others, unseen, potentially evolutionary or regressive, depending on the strategies of interaction. The main intellectual task of the game Thermopylae is to foster the mental faculty of sociological imagination, knowing that today the challenge of the social sciences is above all to make people cultivate and recognize personal styles of action and relationship, rather than suggest infallible recipes.

6.2. Unfolding

Three groups of people ranging from four to seven members maximum are formed. A specific scenario is distributed to each group that will determine the socio-historical context specific to each group. Below are the three scenarios to be assigned distinctly to each group:

Group 1. Scenario A

In 480 BC, you are the citizens of Athens, a wealthy and flourishing merchant city of ancient Greece that sits on a plain in the center of Attica. Your wealth is envied by many peoples near and far. At the walls of your city, you see an encampment of Persian troops. Their numbers are small for now, but they will soon increase. You must decide what action to take.

Group 2. Scenario B

You are the generals of the Persian army. The Persian Empire in 480 BC is the largest and most powerful empire to date, stretching as far as the Indus River in the east and as far as Thrace in the west. You have an outpost of your own encamped in front of the walls of the rich and flourishing city of Athens. The distance between the outpost and the bulk of the army is considerable. You must decide what action to take.

Group 3. Scenario C

In 480 BC, you are the citizens of Sparta, a thriving military city of ancient Greece located in southern Peloponnese. Your community banquets and the training of your army are admired by every inhabitant of Greece. At the walls of Athens, a well-known Greek city, your rival, an outpost of Persian troops, is encamped. Their numbers are small for now, but they will soon increase. You must decide what action to take.

Step 1. First Group Meeting (Twenty Minutes): What Is Your Strategy?

Each group can use this unit to decide, in secret from the other groups, what strategy and tactics to adopt throughout the exercise, and what actions to take based on their strategy (making alliances, waging war, seeking peace, stalling for time, etc.). During this first phase, group members will need to elect a champion and an ambassador. The history of diplomacy distinguishes

FIGURE 6. The First Arena.

between the *nuncio*, one who represents the prince but cannot negotiate for him, and the *procurator*, who could negotiate for the prince but not represent him in ceremonies. The modern term *ambassador* combines the functions of the original roles of nuncio and procurator. In the later stages, the ambassador, in fact, would be free to participate in the activities of the other groups, gathering and providing information, opening secret negotiations, etc. (see second group meeting).

Step 2. First Arena (Ten Minutes): The Meeting between Champions.

Each champion meets in the arena to negotiate his or her action with the others, and the confrontation begins. Only the champions can speak at this stage. The others sitting behind them may not speak under any circumstances. Turns to speak are governed by the spontaneous dynamics of the arena alone. At the end of the arena, the conductor writes the actions taken by each individual champion on a blackboard: reprisals, acts of war or peace, alliances, or proposals, etc.

Step 3. Second Group Meeting (Fifteen Minutes): Ambassadors at Work

The groups' task is to continue the previous mandate, taking into account what happened in the first arena: to redefine their strategy, content, and

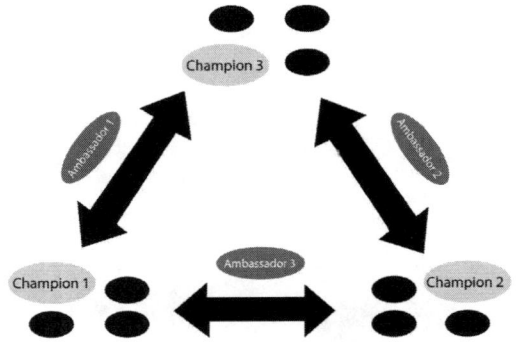

FIGURE 7. The second group meeting and the ambassadors at work.

priorities according to the different positions of the other groups. The group is free to organize itself as it sees fit, even to change its champion or not to present anything in the next arena. In the latter case, the group will arrange itself in its own circular sector, but without occupying the champion's chair. At this stage, the ambassadors enter the scene, who from now on, at any time, can stand up and participate in the work of the other groups to solicit, collect and make proposals, give and receive information, and observe the work of the other groups. No one can refuse to accommodate an ambassador, who cannot stay in a group for more than five minutes. No group can host the two ambassadors of other groups at the same time.

Step 4. Second Arena (Ten Minutes)

The champions' task is identical to the previous one, but in this phase the ambassador can request a time-out to stop the confrontation and consult with the group and the champion. This possibility opens up another level of negotiation between the groups, making communication more pressing and the outcome of the exercise unpredictable. Again, at the end of the arena, the presenter writes on the board the actions taken by each individual champion.

Step 5. Third and Final Group Meeting (Fifteen Minutes)

The task of the groups is identical to the previous one. Also at this stage the ambassadors are free to move into the other groups.

Step 6. Third and Final Arena (Twenty Minutes)

The activity of this last arena is identical to the previous one. At the end of time, the conductor sanctions the end of the exercise and summarizes the positions that have emerged, the agreements that have been made, the actions taken, and the forms of conflicts and agreements that have occurred.

Step 7. Concluding Plenary (and/or Reflection Groups)

This phase involves guided and shared reflection among the trainers and exercise participants. The plenary is intended to foster the process of cognitive abstraction, from experience, around the general conceptual nodes of the theoretical assumptions underlying the political and social dynamics of conflict and diplomatic negotiation.

6.3. Competition and Strategy

The fundamental methodology of Thermopylae is inspired by the prisoner's dilemma, which is a noncooperative, full-information game proposed in the 1950s by Canadian-born mathematician Albert W. Tucker. The dilemma can be described as follows: two prisoners are accused with circumstantial evidence of committing a robbery. The police arrest them both for aiding and abetting and lock them in two separate non-communicating cells. Each prisoner can choose between confessing to the incident or not confessing. They are given the following information: If one confesses and the other does not, the one who confessed avoids punishment, and the other is sentenced to the maximum sentence. If both confess, they have a sentence reduction. If neither confesses, they have a minimum sentence to serve. The best outcome for the two (pareto-optimal) would be for them not to confess, but this would not represent an equilibrium situation (the so-called Nash equilibrium). The best strategy would be for one of the two to confess and the other not, but the equilibrium situation in this noncooperative game, however strongly counterintuitive, is for both to confess. Indeed, suppose that the two have decided not to confess: they now find themselves locked up in two different cells and wonder whether the promise not to confess made by the other will be kept. It will be remembered that if one prisoner does not fulfill the promise, that is, if he confesses but the other naively continues to keep silent, the former will be released. There is thus the dilemma: to confess or not to confess?

The game of Thermopylae has similarities and differences to the prisoner's dilemma. The main analogy concerns the basic question posed by Tucker's dilemma, namely, what are the conditions, more or less rational, that favor cooperation or competition in a structurally competitive environment? There are essentially two main differences, and they affect the dynamics of the game.

The first is that there are three players in the game and not two. The presence of the third introduces the sociological category of the spectator, or generalized other, which immediately sets the horizon to be considered in a scenario that transcends the dyadic relationship. The presence of a third actor on the scene of interaction makes the game of alliances, coalitions, and betrayals much more complex and unpredictable. On the other hand, we have had occasion to consider in the introductory chapters how significant and indeed decisive the figure of the generalized other is in the very constitution of the sociological game.

The second main difference is that simulation occurs by repeated and communicated steps over time, which progressively introduce new information that changes the horizon to be considered. Time activates the dynamic of circular reciprocity between action and information. In fact, each group can communicate its move, initiating a structured course of action that changes the participants' situation, more or less visibly. Each move, even the one least intent on revealing anything about the implementer, provides information to the other groups. In a circular and reciprocal way, and in a more or less conscious way, each group changes favorably or unfavorably its own situation and that of the others by providing information. Nevertheless, the benefits offered by the course of action outweigh the price to be paid for the information (Osborne & Rubinstein, 1995).

6.4. Strategic Interaction and Violence

Mutual Interaction

In considering the scenario, the group realizes the need to evaluate the other players' views of the overall situation. The group will assess the other players' determination to carry out the game, the state of information they have, and the ability to create lasting alliances. The ability of the champions and ambassadors, in particular, will be assessed from their aptitude for evaluating from the perspective of all parties, their ability not to make it a personal matter, even when they will inevitably be under pressure to make choices, and their ability to dissimulate, putting themselves in the shoes of others. Courses of action will thus be acted out in light of what subjects imagine others imagine about them.

Regulated Competition

The essence of regulated competition is closely related to the mutual interaction between actors, that is, the fact that decisions made by any one of them depend on the prior decisions of other actors. Based on the alleged conduct of the other, each group feels entitled to claim its own security and the realization of its own courses of action. Feeling entitled to do what one believes is right for oneself leads to the unfolding of risky relational dynamics, either out of fear of losing the advantages gained or simply out of inertia. In a situation of regulated competition, the problem is to establish the balance point that applies to all. For no group will give up what it considers right for itself unless everyone is willing to step back, but there is no reason for anyone to undergo such deprivation; that would mean exposing themselves as prey rather than appearing to be a group seeking peace. For this reason, there is no "dark force" with coercive powers that strictly determines the social action of the group, but it is the competitive dynamic that fuels the vicious circle.

Cooperation

Cooperation among different groups would produce greater benefits, but the absence of a referee and common rules of behavior makes the choice to compete strategically less risky. In the event that the groups were still able to assess their potential complementarities, in this case the main problem would be not so much the choice of moves by the players (who could agree in advance on their respective moves), but rather how to allocate the benefits of cooperation (Sennett, 2012).

Strategic Interaction

As we have seen, Goffman's thesis is that in reciprocal face-to-face relationships there are aspects of calculation and manipulation, more or less conscious, similar to those that are needed, precisely, in a game (transmission of information, naive or unintentional moves, masking moves with related covert operations, unmasking moves, counter-unmasking, pretenses, dissimulations, inspections, etc.). In any social life situation, we can find someone capable of profiting from the evaluation of another's moves, but we can also find those who manage to manipulate this process more generally, making manipulation not only their way of life, if one can call it that, but also their main virtue, even their profession.

Self-fulfilling prophecy (Merton, 1949), or self-determining prophecy (Watzlawick, Beavin & Jakson, 1967), is a belief or omen that, by the mere fact of being made explicit, makes the supposed, expected, or predicted event come true, thus validating its own veracity. The idea of self-determination is an extension of another well-known formulation by American sociologist William Thomas that "if men define certain situations as real, they are real in their consequences." A classic example relates to the workings of the financial market, whereby if there is a widespread belief that a crisis is imminent, investors tend to lose confidence and may start selling most of their stocks, actually causing the crisis. With regard to the dynamics of war, an example is preemptive strike, that is, when there is a widespread suspicion of an imminent attack by the enemy, so the decision is made to attack in order to anticipate the opponent's moves, actually provoking the enemy's attack.

Sociological Imagination

In 1959 Richard Wright Mills wrote *The Sociological Imagination*, an epoch-making essay devoted to each individual's ability to "see and evaluate the great context of historical facts in its reflections on the inner life and outer behavior of a range of human categories" (p. 15). His thesis is that there are points of intersection between biography and the history of a society. One of the points of connection are the implicit theories that social actors have of the society in which they live. They imagine, in a more or less conscious and systematic way, how a social system, an organization, or a network of relationships works.

The most fruitful distinction by a sociological imagination is that which differentiates and connects, at one and the same time, personal difficulties and problems of social structure. War, for example, presents the individual with a series of problems that he or she will have to know how to deal with and that will depend on his or her abilities: how to survive or die with honor, how to make the violence stop, etc. The structural problem, on the other hand, will be related to the causes, the enemies' choices, and the effects the war will have on his or her daily life. To think that war depends on a subject independently of the historical scenario is, no matter how skillful and competent we may imagine our subject to be, an absurdity.

The Secret

Every relationship experiences a dimension of secrecy, which is an integral part of relational competence itself. Even in the frankest relationships, the discourse that unfolds between subjects is such that it sets up some things while concealing others. Psychoanalysis has worked assiduously on this condition. Only in a social dimension, however, the secret reveals the consistency of the discourse, just as the shadow gives the perception of the three-dimensionality of real objects. In the social game, the secret is the conscious trick, the one that enables a group to negotiate safely with the opponent, to manipulate him, or to defeat him with a bluff; nevertheless, the secret, however manipulative and strategic, does not exhaust the largely unconscious transcendent dimension of the effects of the action itself, the unnoticed background that regulates the decisions and strategies of the subjects. It is the "not known" that acts in social practices, that keeps them alive and conditioned. The skill of the conductor will therefore also have to focus on this deep layer of participants' moves, which show how intention is but a superficial facade of a very rich mass of constituent elements of subjectivity (Foerster, 1984).

Violence

Humanity's violence not only belongs to a remote and natural past, such as permanent wars in archaic societies, but also arises from an internal and always possible outcome of social relations, as recent civil wars and international war crises highlight. The real problem is to understand how and why violence is always a possible outcome of social relations, keeping in mind that, depending on the ways in which we explain violence, we can legitimize it, nurture it, or misrecognize it, etc. Therefore, it is important to take a critical approach to many scientific explanations of violence, also widespread in the common way of thinking, which use apodictic principles (psychological interiority of the individual; biological nature; or the social, family, group environment) as opposed to the actual specific and locally situated dynamics generative of violence.

The Ideology of Victory

"Justice flees from the camp of the victors" (Weil, 1956). Thermopylae is only ostensibly a war game. In reality, it poses profound and disturbing questions about the belligerence of social relations, where the tenacity and delicacy of women and men are repressed in favor of an uncontrolled and often unstoppable anxiety for enjoyment. In the game, these contradictions can be brought to light, positing, for example, the instance of victory as the general humiliation of the vanquished and the victor, as the defeat—therefore—of the group's social potential. This, on closer inspection, is a nonviolent teaching, of which games can only be a faint shadow. The ideology of winning at all costs still seems to be the dominant one. Perhaps a game in which there are neither winners nor losers can be a good antidote.

CHAPTER 7

Polis

Participation and Skills

POLIS IS IN MANY WAYS THE PROTOTYPE OF THE SOCIOLOGICAL GAME, not only because, from a "registry" point of view, it is the first-born child of our experiments but also because it crosses and concerns instances, contexts, models, and issues that are of specific and exquisite sociological relevance. It is concretely a group training exercise that aims to enhance the socio-communicative skills of those who work in various capacities in the field of educational, helping, and care relationships: teachers of various school levels, educators, trainers, sociologists, social workers, psychotherapists, social animators, doctors, nurses, managers, and so on.

More specifically, Polis aims to develop participants' attention to the circularity between different levels and aspects of the broader communicative processes in which they are immersed on a daily basis:

- circularity between micro- and macrosocial relations, that is, between interpersonal dynamics and the dynamics of broader organizational, community, political, and social communication;
- circularity between interactive practices and representations, i.e., between the reciprocities (positive and negative) in which we are

engaged with moment-to-moment immediacy and our images (personal and social) of the contexts in which we find ourselves acting and interacting.

The methodology is participatory and cooperative. It triggers an interactive and community dynamic that:

- solicits collaboration among participants and continuous adjustments for the production of new information and events;
- connects the training activity itself to local contexts, seeking to respond to the demand for meaning emerging from the crisis of institutions and social organizations;
- establishes a dialogue between the knowledge produced by the social sciences around ongoing transformations and the concrete dynamics emerging through the exercise;
- promotes analysis and change in patterns of thought and action.

In its typical version, Polis requires a maximum of forty-eight participants for a full day (eight hours, including intervals), but it goes without saying that different adaptations are possible depending on the context (between sixteen and forty-eight participants, between four and eight hours, or even multiple days). The game consists of the activation of a shared decision-making process. A process to which various "social agents" contribute, interacting with each other, each impersonated by a small group of participants, who are assumed to be present in a given territory—agencies, authorities, services, companies, professionals, social groups, classes, and generations, etc., according to a different mix each time. The course of the day is marked by a regulated alternation of group meetings and moments of meeting between the groups, called, "agora"

7.1. Why the Name *Polis*?

In the Greek *polis*, as is well known, there is the common symbolic space within which the encounter between various "private" desires/interests and "public" sphere—the square or the *agora*—takes place; in other words, the different, necessarily heterogeneous, and conflicting points of view are confronted by their incessant re-inclusion in a shared horizon of meaning, capable of transcending them. The heart of the city is the square; being a citizen means being willing to participate. The connection between politics and play is, from this point of view, very obvious.

Politics is, however, in a situation of almost permanent crisis. The very substance of the polis has "liquefied," to use a fortunate sociological image (Bauman, 2000, 2001), and the symbolic space of the square has shrunk until it has become almost exclusively a place of ostentation and consumption, according to the well-known drift of gentrification. Learning challenges, as crucial as they are unprecedented, have been issued for several decades to our civil coexistence and thus to our educational processes.

If the totalitarianisms of the twentieth century had annulled the space of public life, from above, colonizing the worlds of everyday life and absorbing them into the sphere of control, the processes of massification of contemporary hyper-mediatized societies threaten it dangerously from below, colonizing the public sphere and actively contributing to eroding its autonomy. Increasingly intimated subjectivities; the daily pursuit of profit; aspirations for self-realization within homogeneous and self-referential social circles; the "pre-political" solidarities of the group, the clan, and often private social enterprise pervade a public sphere increasingly emptied of shared and binding meaning, increasingly resembling a media plaza for frenetically elusive, narcissistically self-contemplative gatherings (Dupuy & Dumouchel 1979). The emphasis on individual self-assertion fuels the separation between the individual actor and the set of social relations and institutions that guide his or her actions. From modernity, social actors have inherited an abstract conception of the individual, which leads to the devaluation of relational and societal points of reference that are indispensable to personal self-actualization and paradoxically ends up denying individual concrete subjectivities.

The issues posed by the crisis of the polis are ignored or underestimated, it seems to us, by much of the demand and supply of education today associated, directly or indirectly, with the word "communication." Mostly, this word evokes separated microsocial or separated macrosocial domains of experience. That is

- separated interpersonal, "psychologized" realms: the now stereotypical question, "How do you communicate better with the other (client, user, patient, etc.)?"
- areas, on the other hand, generically collective, "marketized": the no less stereotypical question, "How do you persuade people (consumers to be seduced, citizens to be educated, etc.)?"

In both cases, Polis's social mediation, or rather its dramatic liquefaction, does not seem to be an issue. And communication is reduced to a mere tool to achieve goals of various kinds, in the relationship with others; goals predefined by those who act, regardless of communicative involvement, in the tragic self-referential illusion that the organizing principle of one's practices and thoughts is enclosed in the individual exterior, or in that of one's own separately grouped, corporate, associational, and "pre-political" "we"—and that "the rest" is up to others, out there . . .

7.2. From the Crisis of the Polis to the Polis Game

Such a representation of the contexts in which one finds oneself acting and interacting produces a kind of schizophrenia, whereby the interpersonal communicative discomforts and conflicts experienced by people on a daily basis are thematized separately ("psychologized"), as opposed to the "big" social, economic, cultural, and political issues. We gradually become more and more blind to the vital circularities that always—beyond our being aware of them or not—intimately bind our daily intersubjectivities with the dynamics, structures, and events of the "big world."

The Polis game is a small attempt to swim against the tide, so to speak, by explicitly thematizing the crisis of social-mediation spaces as a crucial issue of our time and our daily practices; a crisis that educational, care, and helping services and professions cannot simply denounce, but rather are challenged to take on as an issue that directly influences their responsibilities, their representations of the missions that define them, their organizational modes, and their most habitual practices.

The gradual emptying out of meaning of the political-institutional systems that two centuries of democracy had laboriously consolidated is an irreversible process, a consequence of the so-called processes of globalization, and it is of little use—if not worse—to blame the professional and organizational difficulties on their admittedly undeniable shortcomings or their conspicuous self-referential drifts (the privileges of the "caste," which have now become an expiatory stereotype). The exit from the senseless drifts of political-institutional systems is today without a shadow of a doubt dramatically urgent, but it does not have the slightest chance of happening concretely, we believe, if the educational, caring, and helping organizations and professions, in turn, do not thematize their own exit from technical-professional value closures, to consider themselves responsible also for what happens out there and for the resilience of the democratic fabric of society.

We are well aware, of course, that the Polis game is mouse-sized compared to the mountain of problems that these preliminary reflections were intended to raise. However, the occasions on which we have been able to experiment with it, each time redefining and enriching it, comfort us in the feeling that the seeds it leaves on the ground are fruitful. We therefore dare to offer in public an initial presentation of this sociological game, in the hope that it may encourage others to continue in this direction and suggest developments and enrichments.

7.3. Representing and/or Building

While group animations often bring reflection to the psychological, psychodynamic, or group level, aiming to bring out awareness of aspects of interaction that tend to be ahistorical (unconscious defenses, power conflicts, collusions, alliances, group dynamics, boundaries between people and roles, and so on, peculiar to human beings in general), Polis aims to bring out the relevance of the socially situated components—contextual, socio-historical, and socio-cultural—present in each and every interactive exchange: institutional and organizational roles, the groups to which they belong, the purposes that the different actors aim to achieve, and the management of the structural resources available to them (time, information, and materials). More precisely, Polis aims to bring out the representations, personal and shared, that act as an active and creative filter for each and every gesture made in the context of action: representations of one's own role, the role of others, the organizations to which one belongs, the larger social network of which these organizations are a part, and the social worlds within which professions and organizations are precisely situated.

The theoretical assumption implicit in this emphasis on the sociological character of play is the socio-constructivist idea (Pearce, 1989) that our representations (in a sense similar to that developed by S. Moscovici, 1984) strongly influence our actions in forms that remain far more unconscious than we citizens of modernity tend to believe—influenced as we are by that "Cartesian" representation of ourselves that assigns epistemological primacy to consciousness, separating it dualistically from the emotions and relational contexts in which we are immersed (Bateson, 1972). The Polis game aims precisely at fostering knowledge of the representations that, mostly *sans le savoir*, we enter into the dynamics of communicative interaction actively contributing to giving representations the forms they concretely take in our eyes.

7.4. Interacting and/or Imagining

The rules of the game, as we shall see, clearly define the structural boundaries of actors' participation and the spatiotemporal rules of their interaction. From these initial conditions, the expression of different personal and group systems, the modalities of negotiation, and mutual influence in the formation of decision-making are left to the free initiative of the actors. The persistence of the original structural frames of professional, organizational, and institutional matrices naturally constrains the context of interaction, but the exercise highlights and enhances above all the autonomous social making, hic et nunc, of the processes of meaning attribution, evaluation, and decision-making.

Participants experience times and relationships by elaborating shared meanings and knowledge. Personal and group narratives change in the course of decision-making through mutual influence. By focusing their attention on the circularity between cultural repertoires and social action, people can become aware of the situated and contingent character of their actions, learning to modify their feelings of group membership and their individual positioning in group dynamics of inclusion/exclusion accordingly. Polis thus brings out different stories each time, which grow by themselves, by staging interactive events that reproduce lively "samplings" of the actual daily social dynamics in which the operators are usually immersed, and at the same time, for the most part, too caught up in daily emergencies to be able to stop and reflect on the reasons for their communicative malaise, involutional conflicts, and professional and organizational discomforts that not infrequently lead to disaffection and burn out. Through Polis, in short, a sociological laboratory is constituted in which the participants, interacting with the trainers, assume the position of social researchers, that is, of self-reflexive observers of the "real" society of which they are a part, at once as persons, as operators, and as members of organized services.

The exercise thus also becomes a process of inquiry in which the production, collection, and reworking of information take place in a circular and reflexive way starting from the reality being analyzed. The training experience constitutes at the same time a research experience: around the anthropological assumptions of a certain territory and the professional cultures that are part of it; around the logics that govern its strategies of action; around the social systems that are taken as priorities; and around the critical issues on which one chooses to invest time, energy, and attention. The reflexivity activated through such a laboratory is knowledge that comes alive in context, starting from different worlds of experience and representational filters, which become for each participant evolutionary challenges, urges to proceed beyond what they already think, and a stimulus to integrate the cognitive process of abstraction that has as its unitary "thinking" subject—completely unprecedented for each of the participants—the "community" established by the agora itself.

7.5. Before Polis

Polis requires a fairly large classroom with movable chairs. The team of trainers is optimally composed of three people (variable depending, of course, also on the number of participants). The steps to prepare the actual game are as follows:

1. Self-presentation of the trainers and participants.
2. Purpose: The trainers present the objective of the day and distribute a sheet of paper to participants with the schedule of the work.
3. Game content: The trainers assign a decision-making task that will activate the Polis dynamic. To be effective, the task must be simple and involve a sufficiently general theme to allow the widest expression of opinions, language, and feelings. For example, for a collective of health workers, answer the question, "What do we WANT for a better healthcare system?," or, for a collective of teachers or students, "What do we WANT for a better school?" The verbal voice WE WANT is capitalized here to emphasize that it is important to engage participants on the level of more fundamental preferences, desires, and more general goals. Finally, it is necessary to facilitate discussion on everyone's understanding of the meaning of this task and to check consensus on the possibilities of implementing the exercise.
4. Formation of "social" groups: A picture of possible social agents in the area (professionals, services, users, politicians, administrators, ethnic groups, social strata, families, etc.) to be impersonated during the decision-making process is presented to the collective. Each social agent will be impersonated by a group, which will have to come together to decide how to impersonate it. That is, it will have to decide, negotiating internally, how that social agent will respond to the question/task of the exercise (see item 3 preceding), then assigning a spokesperson to present the response to the other groups (see item 5 following).

    Groups should not be less than five and should not exceed the number of six participants. Groups will be formed spontaneously, respecting only the constraint in the number of players, which must be the same for each group. People will be asked to make an individual choice with respect to some social agents and to decide freely, negotiating with other participants, on memberships. By the end of this phase, a group will have been formed for each social agent. To be effective, this phase requires prior reflection by the trainer on the social roles relevant to the target area context.
5. Classroom layout: A large classroom with movable chairs is required. The collective will arrange itself circularly, divided into the various groups/

agents, and each group will occupy a pie-shaped sector). The vertex of each "slice" faces a hypothetical inner circle that remains empty and gives body to the symbolic space of Polis. The vertices of the individual pyramids, facing the Polis, will be occupied by the spokespersons of each group, who will display a sign with the name of the agent represented. The other chairs are arranged behind the spokesperson, pyramid-like, to allow group members to participate.

7.6. Unfolding

1. First meeting of the groups (fifteen minutes, strictly). The groups meet to decide on a unified answer to the question/task, which will be reported by the spokesperson to the other assembled spokespersons according to the arrangement in. They may meet anywhere in the room (even in one of the "pie slices," or in other contingent spaces).
2. First agora (twenty minutes, strictly). Groups take their places in their assigned sectors. Each spokesperson presents his or her group's response to the question/task, and the discussion begins. Only the spokespersons may speak at this stage. Other participants may not intervene in the discussion in any way. The trainers, placed outside the circle, merely observe the unfolding of the dynamic, and one of them, who is designated as the conductor, intervenes only to remind them of the discussion times, which must be strictly adhered to. Turns to speak, presentation, and discussion times are governed by the spontaneous group dynamics alone. At the end, one of the trainers, designated by the team, briefly highlights some social dynamics (different weight in the discussion of social agents, marginal positions, etc.).
3. Second meeting of the groups (fifteen to twenty minutes). The task of the groups is a continuation of the previous one, taking into account what happened in the first meeting: To redefine the contents and priorities that answer the question/task. The group is free to organize itself as it sees fit, including changing its spokesperson or not showing up at the next assembly. In the latter case, the group will arrange itself in the Polis in its own circular area, but without occupying the spokesperson's chair.

4. Second agora (twenty to twenty-five minutes). The task of the spokespersons is identical to the previous one, but at this stage each member of the group may speak under their breath to members of the same group, including their own spokesperson. During the assembly, the spokesperson can request a time-out to consult with the group. This possibility promotes effective decision-making by making communication more pressing. Also at this stage, the trainers, in addition to observing the unfolding of the social dynamic, must strictly enforce the timing, without intervening on the merits or to influence the manner of discussion and turn-over of the floor, and comment briefly at the end, again, on what has taken place. Finally, the floor returns to the groups for the last time (but depending on the contexts and time available, one may stop at the second meeting).
5. Third and final group meeting (fifteen to twenty minutes). The task of the groups is the same as the previous one.
6. Third and final agora (twenty to twenty-five minutes). The business of this last assembly is identical to the previous one. At the end of the time, the conductor sanctions the end of the exercise and summarizes the positions that emerged, the dominant and minority cultures of the assembly, and the forms of conflicts and agreements that occurred, without emphasizing the success or failure of consensus on the task addressed but bringing attention to the unfolding of the decision-making process.
7. Concluding plenary. This phase involves guided and shared reflection between trainers and exercise participants. The plenary is intended to foster the process of cognitive abstraction, from the emotionally shared experience, around the general conceptual nodes of the theoretical assumptions underlying the Polis game, which were briefly anticipated at the beginning of the day. In the making of the exercise, events emerge that are both observable and experienced, useful in fostering an understanding of the intimately relational dimension of the identities—of the social agents—that make up the connective tissue of a territory. One step at a time, each can discover that the deep meaning of one's actions does not spring from one's own partial self-referentiality but from one's way of posing to others and from the largely unconscious representations of self and others that actively filter one's actions.

7.7. Trust and Social Identity

The Polis experience is different each time, of course, and each time different themes emerge in the reflection of the final plenary, related to the specific professionalism of the participants, to the organizations they belong to, to the territory of reference, and to the unfolding of the interactive affair over the course of the day. Below we recall briefly, and without any claim to exhaustiveness, some guiding themes that as trainers we propose to keep in mind in the synthesis of the concluding plenary, consistent with the theoretical-epistemological criteria evoked at the beginning.

Taking Care of Trust

Polis places each participant from the outset in the position of negotiating mutual trust with the other group members and with the group as a whole. Such negotiation is fundamental in defining both the affective and relational framework necessary for the course and the progressive approach to the realization of the proposed task. Each person thus experiences that trust is not a condition given once and for all, but an extremely complex and constantly changing relational condition. The richness of personal capabilities and creative expressions that is manifested or not manifested in the course of the exercise depends strictly on the relationship of trust that social actors are able to build among themselves, and not on the sum of individual "incoming" talents.

From the Given Context to the (Socially) Constructed Context

Actors can become progressively aware that there is never a hidden direction of social action. That the context of action, however regulated and socially constrained, is never determined entirely a priori but is constructed through a communicative process made possible by being present, hic et nunc, in a common social space. All participants concur de facto—consciously or not, whether they want to or not—in the construction/reconstruction of shared meanings in the context, making this collective reality an unrepeatable unicum. A construction/reconstruction that influences every aspect of the experience, including "incoming" constraints: individual characteristics, institutional and organizational affiliations, and rules of the game.

From Identity Inheritance to Identity Relationship

Largely unconsciously, each participant is confronted with others not only regarding the proposed decision-making task but also regarding his or her own way of participating in the communicative interaction: that is, not only with regard to content issues but also with regard to relational issues. Throughout the various stages of the exercise, it emerges that individual (personal/professional) identity is not a previously constituted *dataset*, a capital received as an inheritance that one can freely decide to distribute to others or hide in one's backroom, but a dynamic reality, which is formed/reformed through incessant interactions with other actors. It is the flow of glances—dense with expectations, aspirations, memories, hopes—that makes, hic et nunc, the social identity of each actor.

The Paradox of Lack as Competence

Each participant, called upon to put himself or herself on the line without interruption by the very dynamic of communicative interaction, is at risk of exposing his or her own frailties, incompetence, and shortcomings. And thus a participant may experience the paradoxical condition whereby only by acknowledging the possibility of being wrong can he give his best. Only by admitting his own incompetence can he develop new skills. And only to the extent that each social actor admits to himself and to the group his own fallibility does the group develop a shared knowledge that is new to all and more adequate to the accomplishment of the task.

Creation of a New Language

In the incessant flow of interactions involving the actors in play, the part played by each and the shape of the collective process could not take any form without a precise socially shared vocabulary. A vocabulary that, of course, does not exist beforehand, and that must be created and recreated in the midst of the game itself. A language that to a large extent is exclusive, unintelligible to those who have not participated in the Polis game. This allows participants to learn that every single description—of people, events, processes, and relationships—takes shape for each of them only from within a language; that is, that "perceived things" do not come before words but are constructed/reconstructed by words themselves.

Priority of Communication

However, words, with their constructive/reconstructive value, are but one part of a larger communicative process, which also includes gestures, emotions, and the generative force of mutual desires. Participants have the opportunity to experience that the communicative process is a social dynamic broader than any single word or gesture. Wider than the very individual identities that interacting contributes to shaping it. A pervasive dynamic, modulated by largely unconscious abilities—unlike what is mostly understood by the term "communication," which is often reduced to designating a partial and circumscribed moment that would be in the power of individuals to direct in one way or another, as it is in the classic linear emitter–channel–recipient scheme.

Emotions as Social Processes

In the process of joint attribution of meanings, a game of actions and retroactions, of continuous referrals of approval and disapproval, largely unconscious, emotions play a major part. Facial expressions, body postures, gestures, vocal tones, and silences all actively contribute to defining the possibilities and constraints of the communicative context and decision-making process. Participants have the opportunity to experience the fallacy of what is usually understood as emotions, i.e., momentary states of mind that have life in the separate interiority of individual actors, and to grasp the immediately relational and social character of emotions: their arising, moment by moment, from the "mirror play" of mutual gazes and mutual attributions of desires and expectations.

The Game of Social Recognition

The judgment of an action, idea, or motivation to act takes shape through the desire for relational and social recognition. By reflecting on the interactions experienced in the Polis course, participants can raise awareness that each actor pursues his or her own interest or wish fulfillment by imagining the judgment and recognition of others—not by following solely intra-individual criteria and principles (of utility, pleasure, or value), but always by recognizing a priori, consciously or unconsciously, broader moral and social principles that govern his or her relationship with his or her community as a whole, and that take on life and meaning in the midst of incessant communication, both micro- and macrosocial.

Personal Responsibility as a Social (and Aesthetic) Process

Through the incessant communicative interactions, between group and agora meetings, participants touch upon the fact that individual identity exists only as social identity. This means being able to touch upon the fact that personal empowerment is never, de facto, a process of only individual relevance but always relational and social as well—part always of a larger process of mutual co-responsibility. The word "responsibility" is no longer connoted, moreover, by the mere self-imposed "dutiful" tonality but by the aesthetic discovery that each and every interactive event springs from a common "dance" between subjects who co-respond to each other, moment by moment, each according to his or her own style.

Responsibility for the Part and the Whole

In the unfolding of the interactive dynamic, individual prerogatives as well as professional, organizational, social, and institutional affiliations and cultures can be transformed from constraints into opportunities for encounter and resources for the realization of the common task. This creates an opportunity to recognize the vital importance in each social context of the responsibility of each part to the whole. At a time when individuals and individual economic and social agencies are retreating into their respective self-referentialities, in the implicit or explicit expectation that the whole will be regulated by free competition or by superordinate "political" entities, now manifestly in crisis of legitimacy and effectiveness, this appears to be one of the most valuable formative opportunities offered by Polis.

CHAPTER 8

Collapse

Before It's Too Late

COLLAPSE IS A GAME THAT TAKES PLACE IN A SIMULATED SOCIAL environment in the future. The game is intended to enhance the ability of players to imagine new ways of being; communicating; and relating between different cultures, knowledge sets, and skills. It is particularly aimed at young people—and those who work closely with them—to educate and enhance their political capacity to build links between different worlds and cultures present in schools, youth centers, associations, oratories, playgrounds, pubs, discos, and streets, etc. In particular, participants are called to experiment with the construction of new ways of coexistence and other possible ways of being to orient themselves in the social and anthropological transformations of contemporary society. The game consists of interpreting a catastrophic scenario where, in order to survive, it is necessary to design and realize new evolutionary opportunities, integrating reason and creativity, logic and imagination, objective knowledge and hypotheses, data and unsolved problems, and rationality and emotions. Collapse thematizes the different dimensions of change at various levels (individual, family, peer group, community, and society), leading participants to reflect on the social changes in which we are immersed on a daily basis and which prefigure the society of tomorrow:

- change of structures (cultural, religious, legal, and political, etc.) capable of resolving the antagonistic and destructive tensions that society as a complex system generates within it;
- change of social interactions capable of building and maintaining connections between groups, of communicating across space–time barriers, of comparing different points of view on the future, of taking a view that is not necessarily that of the culture to which one belongs, and of multiplying the modes and types of intersubjective relationships and forms of democratic coexistence.

The game uses an active participatory and collaborative methodology to cultivate skills and abilities of foresight-germinability, foreshadowing of scenarios in uncertain contexts, and imagination and elaboration of innovative strategies and actions with respect to novel problems. Specifically, participants have the opportunity to elaborate alternative cognitive paths to social conformity. Collapse helps to

- discover and understand the network of interconnections and interdependencies that characterize the current world;
- acquire the category of social change as a key principle for understanding biological, technological, and biotechnological processes, etc.;
- recognize the element of ecological and environmental risk in a broad sense as a specific dimension of societies with high technological and scientific development;
- and gain a deep sense of multiculturalism as a form of shared participation and responsibility.

A number of at least twenty-four participants is required to play Collapse for a full day (eight hours, including intervals). Depending on the context, different adaptations are possible, even over several days, diluting the time of the exercise. The course of the day, after the initial delivery, is self-directed by the participants, guided by the trainers and some minimal rules of the game.

8.1. Why Collapse?

We have chosen the word "collapse" to denote the physical and social landscape of a catastrophic world whose image, in the game, is inspired by what has—in an age of "collapse," from the Berlin Wall to the Twin Towers, via the ruin-strewn landscapes left behind by wars, earthquakes, and other natural disasters—has now become a fundamental genre in Western culture: the aesthetics of disaster and the looming collapse (Diamond, 2005).

The world is such precisely when it recognizes itself as a finite island in the infinite ocean of the universe. Already the Easter Islanders experienced the tragic realization that their world was finite in terms of economic and ecological resources. Lacking the imagination to explore new geographic and social horizons, they condemned themselves to self-destruction through land impoverishment, massive emigrations, and increasingly frequent and bloody conflicts. After an initial colonization, dating back to the ninth century AD, inhabitants of Polynesian descent began the construction of the famous *moai*, which required the use of an impressive amount of lumber to transport them. Competition among different clans in the production of the rock statues served primarily to enhance prestige and social reputation. The pursuit of prestige, as always, attests to a process of economic and demographic development. However, the achieved prosperity and widespread wealth concealed the risk of imminent collapse due to the depletion of the immense palm forest that originally covered the island and enabled its development. Deforestation was intensified in proportion to the significant increase in population around the fifteenth century. The intensification of competition because of the inevitable reduction and disappearance of timber provoked bloody social conflicts, even to the point of violent civil wars, no longer mitigated by the prestige that had until then been symbolized by the *moai*. It was no accident, then, that the very ancient symbols of the power of clan chiefs were largely torn down by those who had placed their trust in them for imperishable social cohesion. Similarly, the inhabitants of Earth are experiencing, more or less consciously, the finiteness of their world, ignoring other possibilities of coexistence that do not require the massive exploitation of the last environmental resources. Society discovers itself as such on the verge of collapse (Simonse, 2018).

In the play, some of the main analytical categories of contemporary sociology emerge as symptomatology of a society that constantly, almost chronically, measures itself against the limits of its own subsistence. The categories thematized as the game evolves are: risk (Beck, 1986), uncertainty (Bauman, 1995), sad passions (Benasayag & Schmit, 2003), and decline (Sennett, 1976). Risk presupposes taking into the field of view of the present a future (postmodernity) that is already emerging (environmental disaster, terrorist war, energy crisis, and population decline, etc.) in relation to a past (modernity) that is still predominant (industrial production, oil-derived raw materials, state apparatuses, and nationalistic ideologies, etc.). Uncertainty is the general existential condition of an era that laboriously transits between what remains of a modern society and its overcoming; the most obvious feature of this transit is the systematic dismantling of traditional cardinal points (social protections, permanent employment, political organizations, and national identity, etc.). The widespread emotional tone of society, especially in the younger generations, is tinged with sadness and distrust; people are consigned to an exhausting struggle against an increasingly unpredictable world, and, in order to succeed in life, they are forced to relentlessly experiment with new means to derive a modicum of satisfaction from an abnormal context that, overall, is deaf and blind toward them. The social imaginary is recounted as declining: instead of the successful, self-made man, the great Western capitalist of the early and mid-twentieth century, at times cold, callous, and impersonal but striving for social recognition in the public dimension of life, a new human type is being configured, from the yuppie of the 1980s to the financial speculators of the present day—a human type exasperated by the narcissistic realization of its own supposed authenticity, who uses public space to express exclusively the need for his or her own self-realization.

Risk, uncertainty, sad passions, and decline are the key elements to interpret a social system deeply marked by a condition of agony, which can degenerate into collapse (the death of the system and its vital components) or evolve into a form of awakening (the metamorphosis of the system). "Agony," from the Greek *agon*, means "struggle," "competition," that is, literally fighting for the last moments left to live. The metaphor of agony reveals the conflict inherent in social cohesion. What makes life and every manifestation of it valuable lies in its ephemeral nature, in the natural interplay of predator and prey, of life and death that marks every ecology. Similarly, what fosters the sharing of a feeling, a goal, or a value—in a word, solidarity—is precisely what makes social bonding ephemeral: the possibility of conflict is an ever-possible outcome of human relationships that are ambivalent by their very nature.

8.2. An Interweaving of Metaphors

The metaphor of agony is not the only key to understanding the action of the participants in the game. Collapse activates in the participants a wide range of reflections on metaphors related to the future that is emerging in contemporary society. It reveals the priority of metaphors over abstract and decontextualized values. On certain values, in today's society, there is general agreement. Who would be against the environment, life, or the biosphere? Who is not against civil war and violence? These unquestionable values, however, mask deeply ambivalent metaphors. For example, the idea of "saving the planet" may presuppose the belief that Earth is an object in our possession and that its natural fate depends on us. Which is partly true, but it is terribly anthropocentric: not always, not even in the most evolved ecological debate, is the assumption that humans can at all times control the outcome of their actions and events challenged. The analysis of metaphors makes it possible to contextualize the conversations taking place during the game within the broader macrosocial structures: each decision of the participants is told to the others through images that serve the conductor to explicate the overall design of the game strategies; in short, it is a matter of showing how the players' imaginations act by displaying the gap between rhetoric and actions. For example, one can tell about being an environmentalist when it comes to the choices of others, but, when a decision challenges one's own interests, moral qualms often take a back seat. Players, to their surprise, may discover a very different self-image from their stated one, redefining behaviors, roles, and decision-making processes.

Metaphors compose the expressive syntactic possibilities of the players, the horizon of imaginative capacities of those who, by participating in the game, aspire to the construction of a future society. Now, conscious or unconscious, intended or unintended, metaphor is actively constructed within the interactive dynamics that take shape during play. They cannot be reduced to formulas of principle or value ("The society of the future will be supportive" or "The society of the future will respect the environment"). Not that such formulas are false, however, they are not sufficient to account for the metaphors at work in social practices; on the contrary, they end up delegating them to a representative frame function. Instead, metaphors are in place, and their being said, more or less explicitly, underlies the way we imagine social bonding and relations with the environment, specifically the subjective expressions of those who participate.

The power of metaphor lies in its irreducible "non-communicability": one can never say it completely, precisely because every saying is already the outcome of its action. Imagining the environment as "enemy" (hostile nature), "space" (reclaimable zone), or "system" (ecological niche) actively contributes to the definition of the analytical, synthetic, and decision-making possibilities of a subject who, when he takes the floor, assumes responsibility for his action ("I am the subject of . . .") and his partiality ("I am the subject to . . ."). The presence of one or more specific metaphors depicts the deep connection between subjective experience (affective, bodily, reflective) and the specific historical, social, and organizational situation of which one is a part. The purpose of the Collapse game is precisely to recognize that metaphors, when they define interactions, contribute to their factual realization, according to Thomas and Thomas's well-known axiom that "if men define situations as real they will be real in their consequences" (Thomas & Thomas, 1928, p. 572).

8.3. Unfolding

After a brief presentation of the objectives of the game, participants are given the task of reconstructing the future society where all groups must peacefully coexist. It is important to facilitate discussion on everyone's understanding of the goals of the game. Participants, divided into groups, are presented with all the profiles of the communities to be impersonated, paying special attention to understanding the cultural specificities described in the community profile cards. Each profile will be assigned to a group, consisting of at least three people, who will have to come together to decide how to interpret the cultural specificities and how to interact with others. That is, the group will have to decide, negotiating internally, with which identity modes it will respond to the exercise task, then assigning a leader to present the response to the other groups.

Collapse requires a sufficiently large space with movable chairs and a central table. Under optimal conditions, the game should be led by at least two trainers.

Groups of people, ranging from three to five components maximum depending on the number of participants in the game, are formed and arranged at the extremes of the classroom or in different classrooms. Each group then receives the following materials: the "Beginning" and "After Collapse" scenario cards, the community profile card, and the instructions card.

Each individual profile determines the specific characteristics of the community they belong to that survived after Collapse (generic description, strengths, weaknesses, domain scope, and residences). So below are the materials to be distributed to each individual group.

Scenario: The Beginning

The following fragments are from the memoirs of a human trying to reconstruct the scenario and living conditions on Earth before the Collapse.

> It all began in the year 11,988 of the HPE (Hyperindustrial Planetary Era). In the current Posthuman Era calendar, this moment corresponds to the year minus 71, remembered as the year of the Collapse. At that time, Earth had reached its maximum development. Rammstein, the planet's capital, overlooking the Ocean Sea, was naturally destined to become the most inhabited and wealthiest urban agglomeration in the global history of human civilizations. The planet's population, with a steady increase, had peaked through stem-cell cures and biotechnological birth control. An endless throng of humans, spanning hundreds of generations, worked in the offices and laboratories of the new technologies enlisting the help of cyborgs for the most strenuous jobs and high mortality experiments...
>
> The mutants, beings endowed with faculties and powers above the ordinary, the result of more or less accidental mutations that occurred in

the laboratories of the new technologies, ensured that humans kept law and order in the cities and defended them from attacks by extraterrestrials ...

In the Foundation, home of the imperial archives in the capital, the psychohumans, advisers to the emperor, guarded the knowledge, tradition, and morals of humanity. These humans with superior intelligence were assigned the task of enacting the ethical dispositions of the various social communities and guiding their choices in order to maintain the status quo. The psychohistorians also worked on the production and for the proliferation of a rational and purely material discourse on the concepts and things of the world, in stark contrast to the spirituality of the harlequins, "angels" propelling the motions of the soul and creativity, capable of simultaneously presiding over different worlds (the real world, the dream world, the hyperworld) ...

The Skeens, interplanetary travelers and founders of orbiting human space colonies, had signed a pact with the inhabitants of Earth under which they could enlist the help of cyborgs to maintain spaceships and implement communications between their bases ...

The countryside around Rammstein and the other cities of the empire was controlled and cultivated by the Kurgan communities, an extraterrestrial population devoted to agriculture and animal husbandry, on which the supplies needed by the inhabitants of the large urban agglomerations depended ...

Even today, survivors of the Collapse have been unable to understand how this could have happened. In the span of a single year, a drop in the ocean of galactic time, everything suddenly changed, leaving those who remained with the difficult task of rebuilding future society ...

Scenario: After Collapse

The survivors live in the city of Rammstein, what remains of the only urban agglomeration that withstood the Collapse thanks to an advanced technological disaster prevention system. There is no life left on Earth (or, at least, so it is thought) except in Rammstein and the desolate contaminated countryside that surrounds it, where the few Kurgans who escaped the disaster try to derive supplies from land that is now all but unusable for farming and ranching.

The surviving humans, the most exposed to the acid rain and generally deteriorating environmental conditions, have taken refuge in what were once the steadiest pillars of the metropolis, the malls.

Inland, not far from the coast, stationary on an abandoned launch pad, lies a giant, spherical-shaped spaceship built by the Skeens to save the humans from the Collapse. Inside live the surviving Skeens, who have now lost almost all contact with their brothers' space colonies.

The streets of Rammstein are controlled by the cyborgs, still equipped with the latest technological devices for interplanetary and intergalactic telecommunications.

The psychohistorians after Collapse have never left the Foundation, in which they are still refugees and in which they preserve the residual knowledge of civilization and the magical-technological ruins of the HPE (Hyperindustrial Planetary Era).

The harlequins, constantly oscillating between worlds, observe humanity working for survival and manifest themselves only when summoned.

Community Profiles

CYBORG PROFILE

Cybernetic organisms are bionic organisms—the homeostatic and dynamic synthesis of artificial (robotic, computer) and biological elements. They are beings with an extraordinary ability to live in inhospitable environments, enduring in extreme situations. The intimate relationship between man and machine makes them tireless workers but also vulnerable, for, if deprived of regular maintenance and monitoring, they risk their lives.

SPECIFIC TRAIT: pragmatism
STRENGTHS: physical endurance, operational rigor, sense of direction
WEAKNESSES: hyper-emotional, need for periodic maintenance, unable to lie
DOMAIN: technological production (pharmacology, eugenics, domotics, and robotics, etc.)
RESIDENCE BEFORE COLLAPSE: the Rammstein Institute of Technology
RESIDENCE AFTER COLLAPSE: indefinite

MUTANT PROFILE

Mutants are humans with a particular genetic trait that allows them to develop out-of-the-ordinary abilities and powers (telekinesis, teleportation, de-materialization, longevity, molecular restoration, and magnetism, etc.). Since their origin, they have been considered the next stage of human evolution after *homo sapiens*. Because of their extraordinary powers, they were segregated from humans in colonies on the outskirts of megacities. Their long isolation, which ended with Collapse, made them clumsy in social interactions with other groups and unable to provide for their own sustenance.

SPECIFIC TRAIT: creativity
STRENGTHS: superpowers
WEAKNESSES: autistic traits, not self-sufficient, naive
DOMAINS: scientific innovation
RESIDENCE BEFORE COLLAPSE: colonies
RESIDENCY AFTER COLLAPSE: the scientific base of the polar circle

HUMAN PROFILE

The species *homo sapiens sapiens* is relational and social, manifesting an irrepressible desire to manipulate the world around them, seeking to understand and transform the natural environment through technology. Recognizable by their mental abilities, humans have the power to combine technique and knowledge. Biologically susceptible to disease, they are emotional beings with an ambivalent nature: capable of great acts of generosity, they are also capable of acts of overpowering and destroying their surroundings, their inhabitants, and their own species.

SPECIFIC TRAIT: strategic thinking
STRENGTHS: sociality, empathy, curiosity
WEAK POINTS: cynicism, physical vulnerability, self-destructiveness
DOMAINS: politics
RESIDENCE BEFORE COLLAPSE: Rammstein
RESIDENCE AFTER COLLAPSE: indefinite

SPIEGELIAN PROFILE

Spiegelians are an extraterrestrial species with natural mimetic abilities, thanks to which they have been able to expand into the most diverse environments, taking on the most diverse forms of life. Except for the cybernetic one, they can assume any semblance as long as it already exists. Their enormous mimetic power is also their weakness, because, without others to inspire them, they cannot differentiate themselves. Their worst fear is being isolated from other living species.

> SPECIFIC TRAIT: mimicry
> STRENGTHS: adaptation, imitation
> WEAK POINTS: fear of isolation, need for recognition
> AREAS OF DOMINANCE: any except technological
> RESIDENCE BEFORE COLLAPSE: anywhere but the Rammstein Institute of Technology
> RESIDENCE AFTER COLLAPSE: anywhere but the Rammstein Institute of Technology

PSYCHOHISTORICAL PROFILE

They are humans with upper-class telepathic and speculative powers. Experts in the mathematical sciences, they are the founders of psychohistory, the science that can predict, according to probabilistic laws, the future of long-lasting historical and social events. Keepers of the knowledge of all humanity before the Collapse, they lived within the Foundation, where the *Planetary Encyclopedia* was stored. With a convivial and sociable nature, they are entirely absorbed in their research, which makes them eternal children, bearers of boundless knowledge but unable to translate it into concrete actions.

> SPECIFIC TRAIT: logic
> STRENGTHS: knowledge, memory skills
> WEAK POINTS: naiveté, persecutory foibles, lack of practical sense
> DOMAINS: knowledge
> RESIDENCE BEFORE COLLAPSE: the Foundation
> RESIDENCE AFTER COLLAPSE: indefinite

HARLEQUIN PROFILE

An ancient and now extinct lineage of warriors of unknown origins, protectors of life, harlequins are chosen souls capable of moving between parallel worlds, where they receive strength and wisdom with which to nourish the spirituality of living beings predisposed to listen. Of extraordinary strength, they are animated by pure idealism and stubborn endurance. They can intervene in the most desperate situations to restore harmony, but only when summoned by others, never on their own initiative and always in defense of life. Their gift is to be able to assist in any activity of living communities.

SPECIFIC TRAIT: wisdom
STRENGTHS: strength, endurance, harmony
WEAK POINTS: idealism, immobility
AREAS OF DOMINANCE: caring
RESIDENCY BEFORE COLLAPSE: the hyperworld
RESIDENCE AFTER COLLAPSE: the hyperworld

SKEEN PROFILE

They were the first Earthlings to establish colonies in space. After about a millennium, the Skeen decided to sever all political ties with Earth and implement a policy of birth control to sustain a high quality of life, along with the extensive use of robots. We also note their longevity, about four times the life span of an Earthling, so we speculate that they may have actually been descendants of humans selected by a nonhuman intelligence based on their mental characteristics. Be that as it may, the cumulative effects of genetic alterations related to the use of nanotechnology have genetically separated the Skeens from the rest of humanity.

SPECIFIC TRAIT: efficiency
STRENGTHS: exploratory ability, self-determination, leadership disposition
WEAK POINTS: snobbery, poor adaptation, anaffectivity
AREAS OF DOMINANCE: the galaxy
RESIDENCE BEFORE COLLAPSE: space bases
RESIDENCE AFTER COLLAPSE: space bases

KURGAN PROFILE

During the Planetary Era, this extraterrestrial population had little contact with other living species in the galaxy, eventually taking a very marginal role in the affairs of the universe. Physically small, disinclined to exploration and technological innovation, the Kurgans are skilled cultivators and breeders of the most eccentric yet nutritious living species. In the time of the Skeen lord, they were conquered and forced to participate in his intergalactic military campaigns because of their propensity for sacrifice. With the end of the War of the Two Worlds, the Kurgan peoples returned to their placid isolation, maintaining some contact with humans.

SPECIFIC TRAIT: industriousness
STRENGTHS: living with the essentials, self-sufficient, determination
WEAK POINTS: lack of creativity, distrustful, tendency to gregariousness
AREAS OF DOMINANCE: food production
RESIDENCE BEFORE COLLAPSE: planet Kurgan
RESIDENCE AFTER COLLAPSE: wastelands

Instructions

Each group elects from among its members a leader and a delegate. The leader has the power to speak in plenary meetings and is the only one with that power. The other members of the group may attend the discussion but without intervening in any way (any dissonance with the leader should be discussed below in the group). Plenary meetings have an unspecified duration, turns of conversation are free. They are repeated for an unspecified number of times; their purpose is to define the conditions (moral, legal, economic, and ecological, etc.) of reconstructions of the future society. The first plenary meeting, the only one regulated in time and duration, takes place twenty minutes into gameplay and lasts fifteen minutes maximum; it is compulsorily attended by everyone except the harlequins, who may attend only if summoned by at least one community. At least three plenary meetings must be held within the entire duration of the game. To convene them, the request of one leader and the adherence of at least five others is sufficient. The leader who wants to call the plenary addresses the leader/trainer, who in turn interrupts the proceedings and spreads the request to all groups; the groups decide internally—within one minute—whether or not to join the call. This rule applies to everyone except the harlequins. They are obliged to adhere if explicitly called but may not call plenaries. A plenary meeting cannot last less than fifteen minutes. Any group can ask another to host a delegate, who is the only one who can participate in the work of the others and move freely among the groups. The participation of delegates in the group work of the others is subject to the availability of the host groups, which decide freely. In no way can the delegate's presence be imposed. This rule does not apply for harlequins, who may participate with a single delegate in any working group.

8.4. Crisis and Revival

Crisis

Every crisis brings with it a moment of suffering, disorientation, and radical, authentic helplessness: one welcomes within oneself that our world made of certainties has collapsed. What is wrong may concern the self, one's profession, relationships within the organization, or one or more conflicts. All of these have a common characteristic: a feeling of unease and disorientation with respect to future prospects. The term "crisis," in fact, comes from the Greek word *krisis*, meaning "decision." In medicine, the moment of crisis is the decisive one, because it allows diagnosis. Collapse of certainty weakens our chances of foresight, but it is also the possibility of change, of transformation. Symptoms, as long as they remain symptoms, only indicate that something is wrong, but they do not declare exactly what the disease is; crisis is a decisive suffering that could allow the turning point toward a new state of well-being.

Counterproductivity.

The expression "counterproductivity" is from Ivan Illich (1976) and refers to the phenomenon whereby a fundamentally evolutionary procedure turns in the opposite direction once a certain threshold is reached. The social process can exhibit involutional characteristics. The same dynamics of progress and development at the heart of the success of Rammstein's fictional city—thus technological development, the rationalization of life, the liberalization of markets and consumption, the multiplication of opportunities for choice, and the spread of mass communication, etc.—constitute the premises of the crisis that will lead, in the specifics of the Collapse, to the collapse of the system. Counterproductivity indicates the profound ambivalence of social action and its outcomes, which are not only unpredictable but also paradoxical.

Micro and Macrosocial

The nexus between micro and macro reveals a propensity typical of our time, which is to interpret problems of social structuring as if the solutions belong to the individual. Most problems of collective order, as Wright Mills has already intuited, are traced back to the realm of individuals' living spaces and their face-to-face interactions and relationships. The predominant orientation is to give a primarily psychological explanation for a whole series of critical and contradictory situations of a systemic and structural nature. Such "intimation" of social processes is usually so widely diffused that social actors increasingly find it difficult to imagine the spaces of intersection between their private lives and the major transformations of historical and institutional scenarios (Mills, 1959). Especially, if we consider the case of a family, economic, or ecological crisis, it now seems that everything depends on the individual subject and his or her skills, abilities, personal attitudes, and, at best, his or her proximate relationships. The effect of this flattening can be seen, on the one hand, in the gap between individual biographies and the problems of social structuring, and, on the other hand, in the subject's abandonment to solitude and inability to critically interrogate the whole of the society in which he or she lives. There is, however, a very close link between individual choices and major historical transformations; a link that, although difficult to reconstruct in the collective imagination, the play Collapse thematizes.

Transculture

A distinction is usually made in human-rights literature between multicultural, intercultural, and transcultural domains. The first attests to a multiplicity of cultures that autonomously draw the variegated landscape of globalization; the second indicates the intersections, more or less effective, that take place in encounters between diverse groups; and the third shows instead the generation "by graft," if one can say so, of new cultural perspectives, of new possibilities of coexistence—not already mediated by a neutral third party, the so-called cultural mediator—but engaged in a vital challenge, clearly visible in Western cities through the phenomena of social integration carried out by second or third generations of immigrants. Collapse is a play that stages precisely these transitions, starting from an inevitably multicultural situation, promoting the discovery of unprecedented escapes from attitudes of the twentieth century, fraught with nationalistic and ethnocentric traps.

Order/Disorder

The structure of a social group is configured as a continual search for balance between order and disorder; far from being the best and biologically most effective condition, order is actually, exactly like chaos, an ideal point and never reached by life, which indeed, as the evolutionary sciences teach, needs a good deal of redundancy and disorder to build a habitable and lasting dimension. Nonetheless, there is a tendency in organizations to emphasize order as the hallmark of excellence and operativeness to the exclusion of elements of disorder as so many threats or disruptions. This is universally recognized behavior consistent with the rational expectations of the Western mind, but it runs the risk of being mortifying as far as individual creativity and the general life of the organization are concerned, which as such struggles, necessarily, to stand up to its own ideal image. Order is in a continuous dialogue with disorder: a game like Collapse, which starts precisely from a situation of total disorder, helps to show the generative virtues of redundancy and lack of clear references, with a view to a shared reconstruction. The risk of authoritarian lapses and the triggering of delegation mechanisms by players is perhaps one of the most interesting criteria the game can offer for reading the behavior of actors in a critical situation.

Social Conflict

The social sciences have amply demonstrated that the stable and secure social order has very high costs for its members in terms of conflict. Not only is society based on conflict, but, in its absence, what often occurs is a process of domination. It is not uncommon for one set of groups to try to make their interests prevail over those of others, regardless of whether this power struggle is openly manifested. The word conflict calls to mind spectacular events such as revolutions, rebellion movements, and street clashes, yet it is equally concerned with the normal dynamics and processes of dominant and subordinate groups. This dark side of conflict concerns its constitutive ambivalence, with evolutionary or regressive outcomes depending on historical and interactional contexts. In some cases, conflict leads to social integration, helping to strengthen the sense of group membership (Coser, 1956). The search for allies, the centralization of power, and the search for external scapegoats are valid principles when factions of odd strength and power are pitted against each other. Otherwise, when the power between the contenders is equal, the risk of destruction is intensified. In such cases, conflict tends to lead to an escalation of violence that leads to the disintegration of the social bond (Collins, 1975).

Rebirth

Generativity encompasses the plurality of intelligences, knowledge, relationships, networks, projects, creativity, which are present in every social context. The process of value generation today is fueled mainly from below, through the initiative of individuals and groups. However, this capacity for enterprise, innovation, promotion of ideas, projects, and actions, in the form of experimentation, often risks remaining fragmented, dispersed, and, therefore, too weak to activate change. Hence arises the urgency of learning to recognize within each reality those social actions capable of connecting and recomposing the actors involved in the generation of value (economic, institutional, relational, and social).

Ecology of Mind

Collapse, evidently, is an ecological game, in the etymological sense of the term; it is a game about discourse (*logos*) and about dwelling (*oikos*), that is, about the world-environment we inhabit. Eco-nomy and eco-logy are today the privileged fields of the great transformations of society, which have been taking place in recent years. We usually give these events the name of crisis (see supra). Ecology, therefore, is not simply environmentalism. It is, as Gregory Bateson would say, attention to the complex nature of the mind, in the awareness that the environment is not something external and objective, not an inert "thing" just waiting to be taken, contended for, consumed, defended, protected, or safeguarded, etc. The environment, the world, the dwelling, the *oikos* is intimately linked to the mind in a bond that says as much about the health of the planet as it does about the health of the individuals who inhabit it. Caring for the environment and the mind is an imperative that is not just about a political agenda or ideological positioning, it is also and above all about the human condition, which is so because it cares about its own existence.

CHAPTER 9

Zombies

Every Ending Is a New Beginning

LEARNING ABOUT SOCIOLOGY AND CULTURAL PROCESSES THROUGH play. This is the challenge of sociological games. The social sciences study play in at least two ways. A first way involves looking for the correlation between play and culture. Every society has its own games and they can be classified into various types (Huizinga, 1938/2002; Caillois, 1995). The functions of play to be analyzed can be many: socialization, education, vocational training, or leisure. Another way to investigate play is to imagine it as a simulated social context (Boockock & Coleman 1969; Goffman, 1988), where players, by enacting social relations, become aware of their sociological imagination (Fuller, 2006). The analysis here turns to the study of the production of subjectivity (individual identity, ethnicity, political parties, and religions, etc.) and structures (space, time, the body, resources, institutions, and organizations) and the ability of social actors to recognize the links between personal biographies and major historical transformations. This affinity between such seemingly unrelated dimensions "enables those who possess it to see and evaluate the great context of historical events in its reflections on the inner life" (Mills, 1968, p. 18); and, we might add, become actors of change.

The game Zombies is a way of learning the categories of the social sciences, not only through cognitive processes but also, and especially—as is already the case with other disciplines—through affective experience. A sociological game is in fact essentially of a social positioning. This means that participants are put in the situation of reflecting on the space they occupy and their relationships with each other. As we have learned from Norbert Elias's (2009) studies, there is no neutrality in the spatial configurations between people (high-low, near-far, etc.), which have immediate social relevance. At the same time, one's position serves as an indicator of difference; that is, it serves to signal a relationship to the place that others are occupying, without necessarily assuming a given social role. In short, simply occupying a space is enough to influence the course of an action and configure social relations (power, conflict, collaboration, and competition, etc.).

A positioning influences processes of typification or generalization, which are defined within a web of reciprocal relations and from a particular repertoire of culture-referenced norms and sanctions (Schutz, 2018). The generalizations that facilitate our relationship with others in our surroundings are produced and reproduced not only through the contingent positionings of individual participants but also by means of cultural conditioning, cross biographies, and traditions embedded in gestures and recurrent formulas.

Positioning behaviors—practices and strategies of play, as well as the products of these actions and social relations—are constructed during games, each time, not only in unique and unrepeatable ways but also following regularities, which show that even in contemporary society the production of subjectivity and structures is still possible. Subjectivity and social structures are constructed as intersections of discourses, relations, and legitimations, emerging from the typing processes of participants: for example, being a "scientist" or "engineer," rather than "law enforcement," for the player means actively interpreting a role, according to typical and commonsensical ways of thinking, and, at the same time, interacting with what is happening in the course of the game with the other participants, who, in turn, act in the same way, contributing to the definition of the situation, its constraints, and its relational and structural possibilities (Bateson, 1976; Elias, 2009).

9.1. Dealing with Whom?

The game takes place in a simulated social environment in the future. An inter-group game geared toward forming the skills to communicate and to imagine novel solutions in a boundary situation of human and social relations. In particular, participants are invited to experience the construction of new ways of coexistence and survival, other possible ways of being people, for a constructive critique of the social and anthropological transformations of contemporary globalized society. The game consists of interpreting a scenario of extinction of the human species, where, in order to survive, it is necessary to design and implement new evolutionary opportunities, integrating reasons and emotions, objective knowledge and hypotheses, and data and unsolved problems.

Zombies thematizes the different dimensions of collapse at various levels (individual, family, peer group, community, and society), leading participants to reflect on social changes that foreshadow the limits of the contemporary world. Collapse is a society's greatest danger, causing it to plunge into economic crisis, political instability, famine, and pandemic; to change normative and institutional arrangements; and to lose control and hegemony. Social structures and subjects can stiffen out of concern about change and out of anxiety about failing to do so, but collapse can also release a deep desire for change, recognizable in the nascent state (Alberoni, 1977).

The game uses an active participatory and cooperative methodology to cultivate the skills and competencies needed to understand social scenarios and to imagine creative strategies and actions with respect to problems that are not easy to solve. Specifically, Zombies helps:

- to discover and understand the dynamics of social exclusion and processes of marginalization and labeling;
- to acquire the category of interdependence as a key principle for understanding biological, technological, and biotechnological processes;
- and to recognize the element of risk as a specific dimension of high-tech and scientifically developed society.

A minimum number of twenty-one participants and a maximum of fifty-four is required to play. Game time is one to two hours. Depending on the format, in-person or virtual, different adaptations are possible, shortening or lengthening the time of the exercise. The main aspect to be preserved is for it to be a group experience, where the density of group dynamics and social processes are felt.

9.2. How to Play the Game

After a brief presentation of the learning objectives of the game (to develop the different socio-relational dimensions of Collapse), participants are assigned the task of finding a solution to ensure the survival of the human species threatened by the contagious spread of zombies (see The Solution of the Game). It is important to facilitate understanding of the educational purposes and rules of the game by encouraging an initial discussion phase among participants. Participants divided into groups are introduced to the seven protagonist profiles of the game: scientists, common people, doctors, engineers, cyborgs, law enforcement, and zombies. Each profile has cultural and behavioral specificities, strengths and weaknesses, described in the profiles sheets, which the groups must strictly adhere to. The decision to make explicit the specific characteristics of one group's profile to other player groups depends on the choices of the players themselves.

Each profile will be assigned to a group, consisting of at least three people, who must meet to decide how to play their part and how to interact with others. Each group will decide internally on tactics and strategies for action and interaction with others, assigning a leader to present, discuss, and negotiate the choices made.

Zombies requires a sufficiently large space with movable chairs. It is possible to play the game on virtual platforms, creating one virtual plenary room where leaders interact and others assist and as many virtual rooms (or meetings) as there are profiles, to ensure that groups keep their strategic decisions confidential. Under optimal conditions, the game should be led by two trainers and, in the case of distance learning activities, with the presence of a tutor to manage entry/exit from the virtual rooms.

9.3. Unfolding

Groups of people ranging from three to nine players maximum, depending on the number of participants in the game, are formed and arranged at the extremes of the classroom, or in different classrooms, or again, in the case of distance learning, by setting up the groups and assigning each group a virtual room. Each group receives the following materials in hard copy or electronic format: the scenario sheet, the profiles sheet, and the instruction sheet.

Each individual profile describes the cultural and behavioral characteristics belonging to the groups involved in the game (generic description, strengths and weaknesses, and domain scope).

Tab: Scenario

The following fragment is an excerpt from a diary of a woman who tried to reconstruct the scenario and living conditions on Earth in the zombie era.

> The world in which we find ourselves, for many years now, has been shrouded in a kind of silence. It is not really an absence of noise or sound. It is as if everything is muffled by a background buzz, a continuous humming at a very low frequency, that makes it impossible to clearly distinguish signals, to perceive even their origin.
>
> The bustling of the metropolis, the hubbub of the crowd, the traffic, the slogans of advertisements, the laughter of children on their way out of school, the fights, the construction sites, the tachycardiac rhythm of hip-hop . . . there is none of this. The city is a bleak wasteland of abandoned remnants: cars, scooters, motorcycles are left here and there in the middle of streets, intersections, traffic circles. No one can be seen, but only smashed stores, smashed windows, televisions, books, clothes, computers scattered here and there, along with clocks, photographs, electric razors, washing machines, tires, changing tables, chandeliers, bathing suits, beauty products . . . objects of oblivion, things to buy and then forget.
>
> A blinding rays of the sun illuminate the long avenues, shrouded in dense vegetation. Grasses and strange tropical plants have taken root everywhere, invading gutters, courtyards, doorways, windowsills, sidewalks, kiosks. Overhead, the sky is clear, infinitely blue. The day would be beautiful, were it not for that putrid, breathtaking smell. A nauseating sewer smell, stagnating and seeping into every corner, almost palpable, thick, deadly.
>
> In that terrible smell, unbearable for anyone, a multitude of soulless bodies move in unison, never exchanging a glance or addressing a word to each other. In a deafening silence, an undifferentiated crowd walks at a cadenced pace, searching for who knows what. Sleepwalkers wander the city streets, aimlessly dragging their ghoulish bodies. They are the living dead, what remains of the humanity of yesteryear. They have no

self-awareness, or so it seems. They are devoid of physical sensation, unresponsive to stimuli. Their nervous systems are lifeless. They possess, it is true, some reflexes, indeed they see, hear, and smell much more acutely than living beings. They are the zombies.

No one knows exactly what zombies are. Not least because they, the zombies, are unable to explain anything. Humans rely mainly on sight and language to know the world, zombies rely equally on all their senses. They no longer have language and are completely immersed in their new nature. This has developed in them an extraordinary ability to hunt, fight, and feed even in complete darkness.

Their faces are torn by wounds, their bodies mutilated, their arms and legs often amputated. Festering blood tattoos their limping, crawling, but tireless, bodies.

The causes of their origin remain a mystery. Perhaps, the root cause is a virus, produced in a research center or technological institute? In reality, scientific research on the origins of the contagion has been lost along with the last survivors. No survival manual has served to protect Stone City.

At the first signs of contagion, no one imagined the extraordinary scale of the phenomenon for the inhabitants of Stone City, who were overwhelmed by zombies, those beings with a nefarious odor and mutilated bodies, attracted by the slightest noise and moved by an insatiable appetite. The heroes, who went to the rescue of the survivors, then turned into zombies to be eliminated. Will a solution be possible, or will it prove to be yet another trap, gradually confirming, more and more, a terrible fate without hope...

Profiles

ZOMBIES

Zombies are human beings condemned to live lifelessly. They thrash about, moved by a primal instinct that makes them insatiable devourers of flesh, but without being able to taste any of it. They hunger and thirst for blood, not out of the need to feed but out of voracity. Their muscle mass remains damaged, and its effectiveness diminishes after each exertion to a slow and merciless decomposition. They are not immortal: although they have returned from death, their condition cannot be said to be revived. Moreover, another rather disturbing aspect, being technically dead, zombies cannot reproduce. They are infertile creatures. Their sexual organs are necrotic and sterile, and they show no signs of sexual desire toward their species or the living. The only way zombies can reproduce is through contagion. They infect living humans. When the contagion is absolute—their planetary success, paradoxically—they are doomed at some unspecified time to total extinction.

> SPECIFIC TRAIT: non-life
> STRENGTHS: They are unstoppable.
> WEAKNESSES: In terms of physical strength, they are less agile and quick than a living human being. Their gait is slouching and limping. Even without mutilation, even in cases where the muscle tissues have not completely decomposed, they always exhibit a noticeable lack of coordination, which makes their gait typically rocky and shaky. Because of this, they are also unable to run; they can only laboriously quicken their pace when moved by their appetites.
> DOMAIN AREA: Stone City and its surroundings

SCIENTISTS

They are human beings with superior, specialized knowledge. Experts in mathematical, physical, and medical sciences, they are able to predict, according to probabilistic laws, future trends in long-lasting historical and social events. Keepers of human knowledge before the zombie invasion, they live in their research centers scattered across the planet. Gifted with a sociable, convivial, and kind nature, they are entirely absorbed in their research; this makes them eternal children, bearers of extraordinary knowledge, who are nevertheless in trouble when they have to translate it into concrete actions. Their relationship with engineers is problematic because they are judged to be too concerned with solving problems without having an overall vision.

> SPECIFIC TRAIT: logic
> STRENGTHS: knowledge, analytical skills, and creativity
> WEAKNESSES: persecutory mania, lack of practical sense, idealism, and immobility
> DOMAIN: Stone City Research Center

LAW ENFORCEMENT

They are human beings endowed with uncommon strength and discipline. Experts in the arts of combat and security in urban environments, they are able to organize and manage situations of high social disorder. They can intervene in a wide variety of situations by restoring order. They have an autonomous organization and structure, with means, weapons, equipment, and provisions, etc. They are independent of other social centers or nuclei. In general, their function is to ensure public order and safety in crisis or emergency situations. Over the years, law enforcement agencies have established specific departments with specialized tasks, whether for counterterrorism, organized crime, or internal city security. In the most dangerous operations with high mortality risk, they use the operational arm of cyborgs.

SPECIFIC TRAIT: legitimate violence
STRENGTHS: strength, autonomy, and discipline
WEAKNESSES: closed-mindedness, excessive zeal
DOMAIN: Stone City Police Station

CYBORGS

Cybernetic organisms are bionic organisms, that is, the homeostatic and dynamic synthesis of artificial (robotic, computer) and biological elements. They are beings with an extraordinary ability to live in inhospitable environments, enduring in extreme situations. They are immune to any form of viral contagion and do not become zombies even when exposed to their bites. The intimate relationship between man and machine makes them tireless workers but also vulnerable, for, if deprived of regular maintenance and monitoring, they risk their lives. Cyborgs were jointly created by scientists and engineers, who used them for the most strenuous jobs and high mortality risk experiments, while law enforcement agencies used them as an expendable operational arm. Because of this, their relationship with other groups is problematic. The arrival of zombies and their rapid spread has created a chaotic situation, where cyborgs act undisturbed and finally free, but lacking the necessary supports and monitoring.

SPECIFIC TRAIT: pragmatism
STRENGTHS: physical endurance, operational rigor, sense of direction, telecommunications, and applied medicine
WEAKNESSES: hyper-emotional, need for periodic maintenance, and unable to lie
DOMAIN AREA: technological production (pharmacology, eugenics, domotics, and robotics, etc.)

ORDINARY PEOPLE

These are people who do not stand out for special skills or qualities. Insensitive to major historical issues, they manifest a desire to manipulate the world around them, often through technological devices, with an underlying ethical and moral ambiguity. Ordinary people are passionate but have domesticated their passions and aspirations in the quiet of an anonymous life. The arrival of the zombies has worried them and made them anxious to find a solution. Their relationship with the scientists and engineers is one of deep trust. They fear the cyborgs, and they seek protection from the law enforcement.

SPECIFIC TRAIT: strategic thinking
STRENGTHS: sociability, curiosity, and empathy
WEAKNESSES: self-destructiveness, physical vulnerability, and fear
DOMAIN: Stone City

ENGINEERS

They are human beings with superior technological knowledge. Experts in applied sciences, they are able to translate the most innovative scientific projects into reality. Guardians of technology and innovation, they live in technological research institutes. They operate with a high degree of practical sense in the most diverse fields of applied knowledge—biomedical, civil, management, aerospace, environmental, and chemical, etc. Engineers hate projects that are not 100 percent reliable, and they try to eliminate risk from their projects as much as possible. Their relationship with the scientists is problematic, because they judge the scientists to be too abstract and lacking in necessary practical sense.

SPECIFIC TRAIT: technique
STRENGTHS: method, problem-solving, efficiency, technological innovation, and determination
WEAK POINTS: mental rigidity, excessive self-esteem, and sense of omnipotence
DOMAIN: Stone City Institute of Technology

DOCTORS

They are human beings with specialized knowledge about the human body and its care. Experts in surgery, pharmacology, and epidemiology, they are able to take practical action to cure sick people. They operate with a high level of practical sense in the biomedical, genetic, and molecular fields. Their relationship with other knowledge experts, engineers and scientists, is competitive, because they tend to feel threatened by those who do not belong to their guild.

SPECIFIC TRAIT: caring
STRENGTHS: knowledge of the human body, surgical skill, ethics, and spirit of sacrifice
WEAKNESSES: overspecialization, cryptic language, and corporate spirit
DOMAIN SCOPE: Stone City Hospital Center

Tab: Instructions

Each group elects its own leader, except for the zombie profile group. The leader has the power to speak in plenary meetings and is the only one with the power to do so. The other members of the group may watch the discussion but not intervene in any way. Any dissonance with the leader should be discussed below in the group. Plenary meetings have a maximum duration of thirty minutes. After each plenary, the groups will identify from among the players three candidates for zombification, with the exception of the cyborgs, who are immune. The criterion of choice (authoritarian, democratic, or random, etc.) will be determined in the first plenary. The leaders of the groups will have to be chosen last. The zombie group will choose which candidate to zombify and will have five minutes to inform the other groups of the outcome of the decision. The person indicated will have to move to the zombie group. The game will end if all players become zombies, except for the cyborgs.

9.4. The Solution of the Game

The game ends when the participants find a solution to the unstoppable process of zombification. The trainers will communicate that several solutions are possible, but that some specific conditions must be met in order to be implemented. The trainers will not be able to go into detail about the conditions that make the options possible, but they can indicate viable solutions. The options can be: to find a cure (this solution is possible only under the condition of an alliance at least between doctors, scientists, engineers, and cyborgs); to isolate the zombies (this solution is possible under the condition of an alliance at least between law enforcement, engineers, and cyborgs); or to exterminate the zombies (this solution is possible only under the condition of an alliance at least between cyborgs and ordinary people). In the last case, there must be at least two plenaries. In the other two cases, the game ends after the first plenary. Only in the first case (finding a cure) do all zombies heal, even those originally in the zombie profile.

9.5. Between Terrifying Masses and Social Parasites

The experience of Zombies is unique, and theoretical reflection is generated in the interaction and conversations among participants and between participants and presenters. Each time, the socio-demographic, geographical, cultural, and religious specificities of the organizational contexts; the professional or curricular histories; or even personal histories of the players, as well as the dynamic evolution of the exercise, brings out different sociological themes. Although in distinct ways, some guiding themes nevertheless tend to emerge recurrently. Below, we recall briefly, and without claiming to be exhaustive, some of the guiding themes that have emerged with participants over the course of the different experiments.

Social Parasitism

This refers to the exploitation of others. The term "social parasitism" was coined from Marxian studies that probed the social and economic relations between productive and unproductive labor. Over time, the concept of social parasitism has been extended to all areas of life. It occurs when someone exploits the lives of others for their own personal gain. It occurs countless times in the world, taking on the features of the most obvious and invisible normality. It is a mechanism of self-reproduction, which inevitably results in oppression, destruction, and mortification. The terminal figure of the zombie is the one that synthesizes symbolically, and therefore eloquently, this sacrificial mechanism: the existence of the corpse that does not disappear as it should but that undermines civilization in its most trite and trivial habits. This irreducible existence is probably the undercurrent of the Western collective imagination of the last decades. Testifying to this is not only cinema, in which zombies appear in almost every genre—from horror to parody, via cartoons, porn, or even sentimental works (for example, Jonathan Levine's *Warm Bodies*, 2013)—but also literature (think of the fortunes of Max Brooks's books), music, nonfiction, and advertising.

The Undifferentiated Mass

The mass for as long as it has existed, as Elias Canetti (1960) taught us, has always wanted to be more. It wants to grasp anyone who can reach it; by its very nature, it is open, and it has no limits to its growth. The mass is dominated by two power drives: to grow and to survive. The radical and sudden equality of the mass, the erasure of subjectivities and hierarchies, frees it from accumulated thorns, even the most monstrous and self-destructive ones. Similarly, the mass of zombies is plural; there is never one zombie: therefore, it is difficult to imagine an individual, good or bad, with whom to identify. In zombie stories, the viewer or reader is led to follow the vicissitudes of the living human; zombies are undifferentiated.

The Obscene

The origin of the term "obscene" is far from clear, and analysis of the socially and historically constructed nature of sexual obscenities primarily emphasizes its meaning of "impudicity." However, among the various etymologies of this item, depending on the Latin lesson, *obscenus*, or *obscoenus*, *obscaenus*, the earliest—from the Latin *ob* and *coenum*—means mud or slime, in the sense also of "ugly," "deformed," "filthy," "unclean," and only later translated into the moral sense of "impudicity" and "dishonesty." The connection refers, as is evident, not only to the sphere of filthiness and its translated meanings (impudicity, immorality) but also to a further, non-immediate sphere: that of ill omen and the sacred. The obscene, in common with the sacred, possesses the dimension of impurity and stigma (Goffman, 1963; Antonello & Gifford 2015a), closely related to that of sacrifice. And zombies are obscene, stigmatized, and expendable beings.

Zombification

Zombification is a process that empties any gesture of meaning and value, just as consumerism removes value from any object, immediately after its purchase (Žižek, 1991). The now almost classic explanation of the image of the zombie as a metaphor for chronic compulsive consumerism is along the lines of the Platonic allegory: the intellectual comes out of our world, contemplates the truth, and then returns to us to tell us that every time we push a supermarket trolley, every time we gorge ourselves on high-calorie sandwiches, or every time we unload a piece that is in vogue, we are behaving like the living dead, indeed we are living dead. We are so much so that, to avoid thinking about it, we create the shadow-image of the zombie and let this image take the full brunt of our mute and unbearable anguish.

The Scapegoat

Zombies are a violent and plastic representation of the scapegoat; because they are unconscious, devoid of sensibility, hideous to behold, we annihilate them without any mercy and indeed the act of annihilating them reactivates solidarity among living beings. "When Aaron has finished making atonement for the Most Holy Place, the tent of meeting and the altar, he shall bring forward the live goat. He is to lay both hands on the head of the live goat and confess over it all the wickedness and rebellion of the Israelites—all their sins—and put them on the goat's head. He shall send the goat away into the wilderness in the care of someone appointed for the task" (Leviticus 16:20–21). The institution of the most important holiday in the Jewish tradition, Yom Kippur, and in general the elaboration of the most complex and refined mode of social, communal management of guilt and error consists in the identification of an individual to whom precisely guilt and error can be attributed (Girard, 1986). From that moment, the community is lightened, and relationships are recognized as more solid and pleasant; life begins again.

9.6. A Final Invitation

The beauty of sociological games is that participants have the opportunity to question their own identities, exploring other possibilities for action, while still remaining within a fairly protected system, because of the power to interrupt the game and avoid embarrassing ruptures or deepening into their own or others' frailties (Fink, 1957). Each game is, of course, a world apart, unique and unrepeatable. It happens, in the course of the many experiments of sociological games, within a compact social context—a well-defined, distinct, and almost plastic environment—with its own lexicon, tics, and macro dynamics reproduced in miniature. The astonishment of seeing society in action, even with its cultural or social determinants, occurs not so much because of a social structure that reproduces itself independently of the people who compose it, but rather because of the dynamics of the game itself, such that by playing one tends to reproduce in a simulated context, in some ways protected, but for that very reason all the more exposed to the weather of relationships, the social bond constitutive of the group or local community, which takes on new life in the game.

CHAPTER 10

Playing Sociology

Notes on Method and Analysis

THERE IS A SPECIFICITY TO SOCIOLOGICAL GAMES, A PECULIARITY that is exclusive to them. These games develop in participants a sensitivity to the social surface. Of course, surface does not mean triviality. A century of depth psychology, perhaps, has led us to think that the foundation of human action inhabits the abysses of the individual or collective unconscious and can be found in exceptional and extraordinary situations, related to madness, to dreams, and to works of art. In contrast, mimetic theory, with its tradition of theories and research, has taught us, among other things, that, in the surface of the most basic and commonplace human interactions, traits of genius and creativity are condensed and that, in everyday, ordinary life, what happens is not always negligible or stereotypical (Girard, 1978; Antonello & Gifford, 2015b). Therefore, it is useful to experiment with and analyze the different levels of social life in simulated environmental situations, alternating between individual, group, and community activities.

What emerges in the game is the density, the thickness, the complexity of the surface. The guiding themes that we have proposed at the end of the various games are as many indices of salient topics, dealing with problematic aspects of contemporary thought. Although each game has its own uniqueness, and there are irreducible differences among the games, which we also experienced on various application occasions, we were surprised by the recurrence of certain meanings and attitudes. These are not laws of social behavior, universally applicable and generalizable in every context of interaction, but invariants that we repeatedly detected through conducting games and participant observation. Already at the beginning of our journey, we were drawing attention to invariants as a constitutive part of a "grammar" of play, governed by the circular relationship of repetition, strategy, and sociability. Now the discourse, which we had sketched out at the theoretical level, is confronted with social action, with the practices that recur as we put the game to the test of facts.

From these invariants we constructed an interpretive schema that allowed us to give a method of explaining and conducting the various game situations. The schema is not an exhaustive list of the complexity it thematizes; rather it is an orienting synthesis, useful for placing the reflections of the players—a kind of sociological heuristics, a procedure aimed at identifying new phenomena and relations. From suggestions and reflections that have emerged in the course of sociological game practices, it is therefore possible to delve into each individual aspect that could in turn be the subject of a separate discussion.

In the unraveling of the invariants, as we shall see, one will equate the historical and social reality with the ludic and mimetic reality. This, in no way, means debasing or debunking the former in favor of the latter, nor does it mean assuming mimesis to be a hypostasis of empirical reality. Instead, it means that, on the social plane, real and "played" experience develop with the same emotional and relational dynamics. History then teaches how to distinguish one from the other, but this is a task subsequent to play, a task that sanctions a further "seriousness," a consciousness of having played the game of society. It is only after sharing in the game that one can speak of a distinction between game and reality: naive realism deludes itself into thinking it can do without the game, just as fatuous nihilism invests very little effort in asserting that "everything is a game." Reality sequesters and somehow contains the game, embanking it in the exceptional space of its verbal and ritual modes; however, reality itself is embanked by the game; by its gratuitous and paradoxical virtue; its unscrupulous meaninglessness; and its capacity for further referral, for asking for something else, for opening to the other. What matters to us is that the decision to play, as we have seen, is the beginning of social action proper.

10.1. The Framework and Invariants

Managing the complexity of a sociological game entails assuming a particular mode of interpretation, a style, if you will, that guards and preserves the multiple facets and the minimal nuances that are revealed in the playful action. Even in their ephemeral nature, minimal details and contingencies are essential to capture the creative and generative dimension of play. Therefore, it is necessary to prepare an interpretative framework that is sufficiently open, such as to provide criteria that are "hospitable" to events, which neither flattens them into an equalizing generality nor constrains them into a rigid and normative schematization. In this sense, the most established recurring dimensions will be considered, as opposed to the generally ephemeral picture of what happens when we play. These dimensions are a kind of functioning mechanism, which we have been able to observe during fieldwork in exercises and workshops. Following Jean Piaget's perspective, we called them "invariants": in cognitive development, the process of adaptation to the environment takes place by defining, from time to time, a situation of balance between the so-called functional invariants, assimilation, and accommodation (thus Piaget, 1975); similarly, when playing, social groups construct their singularities and specificities from attitudes and behaviors that are repeated with a certain regularity. They always begin with a certain awkwardness, not knowing quite how to move and what to say (see Bewilderment in the following section), and then observe each other and assume from time to time positionings that mutually measure each other (Mimetic Strategies in following). Later, these positionings stiffen, until they configure very precise and recognizable roles and delineate a sort of background of obviousness (Mimetic Automatisms in following). Lastly, the group tends to reconstruct the adventure of its experience, considering the path taken as a series of steps endowed with meaning and linearity, like a shared ritual (Liturgies in following). In any playful experience, therefore, four dimensions are experienced that are characterized by the dominance of attitudes and interactions, for example, of collective function over individual function or of randomness over control. Let us now look at them more closely.

Bewilderment

The first dimension we consider emerges from the mimetic crisis that characterizes every beginning stage of the game, and that is the area of bewilderment. Every beginning is a crisis. The term "bewilderment" contains within itself the confrontation with "wildness," with unfamiliar places. The anthropologist Ernesto De Martino, whom we have already met regarding the concept of "loss of presence," defined "bewilderment" as the feeling one has when one no longer has points of reference. The "end of the world"—into which those who can no longer find their bearings find themselves thrown—is narrated by De Martino in the famous anecdote of the bell tower of Marcellinara: The anthropologist, together with some other researchers, is driving in the Calabrian countryside. The small group is lost, but fortunately they meet a shepherd and ask him for information, which, however, they do not understand. So they propose that the shepherd get into their car and accompany them to the right fork in the road, then they can drive him back to his village (Marcellinara, in the province of Catanzaro). The shepherd accepts with some hesitancy, but, as soon as he loses sight of the bell tower, "the reference point of his extremely circumscribed domestic space, he begins to show signs of disquiet, more and more pronounced, to the point of forcing De Martino's team to take him back (De Martino, 1977/2002, § 271.1).

The experience of disorientation brings about a moment of crisis, which in turn summons the subject's organizational skills. In other words, losing the usual points of reference entails the need to construct new ones. Bewilderment represents the possibility, within any game plan, of radical innovation and the future, regardless of the more or less evolutionary outcome of the changes. Even at the macro-social level, this a phenomenon recurs in the major historical, technological, and cultural transformations of recent years, which have rendered obsolete many of our ways of thinking about and explaining social contexts and the various dimensions of daily life. The collapse of the Berlin Wall, for example, was an improbable historical event that opened up hope for possibilities previously unthinkable in the dominant ideologies' continuous order of cultural homogenization. Who would have imagined such an event, a profound and radical innovation in the order of history? From the perspective of epochal crises, the collapse of the Berlin Wall has an almost absolute emblematic value: it marked a discontinuity from the past; since November 9, 1989, the world has changed face. The new face is different, with all its labors and contradictions. In some ways, we can imagine uncertainty as the rupture of the mechanical and serial order: an unforeseen failure in the "docile robot," to borrow a metaphor from Mills, a flaw in the cog of control, the possibility of the improbable. A similar impression could be drawn from the abrupt change of scenery on a global scale caused by the COVID-19 pandemic. We who are writing this book come from one of the most affected areas in Europe, the province of Bergamo in Lombardy. We remember well and with anguish the days when the obituary pages of the local newspaper went around the world, or the rows of military trucks that in the early morning transported the coffins that the cemetery could no longer accommodate. . . . But beyond the human tragedy that affected the families and biographies of so many people, what characterized this incredible event was precisely its incredibility: The warnings coming from China in the winter of 2019 were not enough. The event, as such, was generally underestimated, far removed, and thought of as something that could never come to fruition in Western civilization. The impact of the pandemic on the lives of individuals and institutions has been enormous and perhaps not yet fully processed, especially with regard to the younger generation. It is another mark of discontinuity that undermines the security of the almost paranoid logic of control.

But this condition of disorientation can also be detected in situations far less dramatic than that of epochal historical events; think also only of the staggering speed with which the development of digital technologies has opened up a generation gap such that younger people are often more proficient than older people in the use of tools vital to communication and coexistence. The fifty-year-old grappling with the new model of smartphone feels all the more out of place (bewildered, precisely) the more his teenage son shows impressive familiarity. The moment of bewilderment is thus connoted with a sense of anguish or anxiety, which can turn into disordered panic (as in the case of the poor farmer in Marcellinara) or into a more constructive and sociologically interesting call for help.

In today's society, bewilderment is intertwined with the dimension of uncertainty. This dimension, however, also evokes scenarios of a completely different kind, which, instead of promoting creativity, deny it any evolutionary value. Uncertainty today is synonymous with precariousness and chronic instability, generating a fear of the future. The desire to predict and control the future tends to turn into an obsession with predictability and planning, which does not tolerate the randomness of existence and history. This obsessive drift, neoliberal and economistic in nature, reduces individuals to helplessness and loneliness in the face of events that are often beyond their control and that they cannot even comprehend. Their biographies are acquiring the same fragility witnessed in world history with its failures and broken promises. The most obvious, and perhaps yet to be discovered, aspect of such an extraordinary short-circuit between biography and history is its declination in generational transition. For the first time in the history of the world (a history, moreover, characterized by an impressive rapidity of change), the youth—the "last-comers," the parvenus of the social fabric—struggle to fulfill their role of rupture, innovation, and creativity (Morin, 1973), but find themselves caught up in the discomfort of those who cannot afford to play, of curricular uncertainty, and of chronic precariousness. In this sense, sociological play that insists on uncertainty can serve as an indicator of the underlying emotional tensions in the group of participants: depending on whether uncertainty is perceived as a factor of anxiety or as an opportunity for redemption, the formation of a social system of expectations and strategic relationships can be observed directly.

Mimetic Strategies

The mimetic subject responds to the bewilderment of events with their competence, which emerges from the relationship between structures and subjects. Mimetic strategies refer to the set of knowledge and skills put into practice by a subject to interact actively and dynamically during each simulation and game. What is learned over the course of a lifetime occurs, primarily and to a very large extent, through imitation, which is by no means a simple operation, but rather accompanies human and social development with a varied multiplicity of constructs. Sociological games are able to show and clarify the way in which the mimetic strategy of learning is configured. It, in brief, can be summarized in three terms: competence, ability, and skill.

Competence is learned in situation, because it is a specific form of knowledge, which is built through action and reflection on practice. Beginning with a chain of trial and error, competence arises as a "trans-contextual leap," Bateson (1972) would say. Therefore, playing becomes fundamental to learning new skills. The area of competence covers skills, knowledge, abilities, and competencies proper.

The etymology of the word "capacity" comes from the Latin *capacitas*, meaning "how much one can take occupy, contain." Capacity consists of taking hold of something—resembling grasping, but also filling—so capacity is an ever-evolving doing, acting, and thinking.

As for knowledge, it is classified into two basic categories: declarative (knowing) and procedural (knowing how to do). Possessing knowledge is not always, as is well known, equivalent to knowing how to teach it. Knowing and sharing one's knowledge are two different forms of competence. Many will have in mind teachers, no doubt very well trained but inept on the teaching side, tottering about in the hope of finding an example, a formula, or a figure that can clarify a passage, in the face of the bewildered looks of pupils. Knowing and making known, precisely, do not coincide, and the high level of one does not always correspond to a high level of the other.

The term "skill" comes from *habeo* and indicates possession. Skill refers to awareness of what one is doing; it is an action whose actor is able to reconstruct the process. For example, knowing how to fix a broken-down car and describing the various steps.

If skills express the shape of our potential being, and abilities indicate our current being, competencies manifest our situational orientations. The etymology of the word *competere* means to "move together, to converge." Competition and competence refer to essentially the same meaning, only that the nuance of the prefix *com-* addresses, in one case, the mimetic conflict generated by a common goal and, in the other, the agreement on the achievement of that goal. A subject can be called competent when, in the face of events, he or she puts into action a plurality of capacities, knowledge, skills (logical, creative, humanistic, relational, linguistic, and/or reflective) that enable him or her to turn the situation around in evolutionary terms. In the sociological game, all this is evident in moments of impasse, when competent subjectivity manages to find a way out in a creative and original way, using the same information and materials available to others but combining them in a novel way. This competence is all the more evident, the more the subject in question is able to communicate it to peers. For this reason, sociological games provide an opportunity to return to participants the mimetic strategies they have activated, unmasking their often unconscious logic of operation.

In particular, in the games Thermopylae and Collapse, these operating logics allow for reflection on the dynamics of violence, their effects in human behavior, and how they are acted upon inadvertently.

Mimetic Automatisms

The connection between structures designed to contain events, on the one hand, and society as a whole, on the other, defines the boundaries of the dimension of mimetic automatisms. Subjects often tend not to pose the problem of the arbitrariness of social life caused by the onset of events, for fear of falling into a regression to infinity, into a succession of questions that never stop (Garfinkel, 1967), so they tend to act in a habitual way, reproducing behavioral patterns dictated by mimetic strategies. During a game phase, it is usual to repeat the behavioral patterns adopted in previous phases, although they are not necessarily useful or beneficial. Indeed, in some cases, such patterns are repeated despite their obvious ineffectiveness.

However, subjects, even when enraptured by the automatisms of their daily lives, have the skills to handle different levels of interaction and questioning. This happens precisely while playing the game. In this case we are not facing a real situation, a real enemy, or a real environmental crisis, but we can behave exactly as if it were, playing between the different levels of interaction and meaning (Goffman, 1963, 1969; Dunkan & Fiske, 1977). Other more complex levels can then be created on this level: training oneself to play, pretending to play, and commenting on the game while playing, etc. All this is possible because there are structures that embrace the different layers and different possibilities for interaction. Subjects therefore can define the situation in which they act by profoundly influencing the context of action and levels of play. But play, as well as any social action, is part of a larger social structure that affects all subjects, and this structure is in turn embedded in a bodily, cultural, and above all, as we shall immediately see, liturgical situation.

The Liturgy

The liturgical dimension recomposes the different dimensions of the game into a unified whole. It emerges as a tension between chance and the aspiration of subjects to govern the arbitrariness of life. This dimension marks the "return to the origin," the resumption of the deep nexus that exists between society and events. From this point of view, society is the compelling response of human beings to the contingency of their mortal condition. Liturgy, with its prohibitions and practices, teaches the subject the rules of coexistence, giving deep meaning to every game. The return to the origin has a strong performative value because it reproduces the initial expression of the game and simultaneously narrates it. Without a liturgical dimension, society falls flat at the level of its structures, devoid of epiphany or manifestation of meaning. The etymology of the term "liturgy" refers to the performance of an act (*ergon*) in a public dimension (*làos*). It is no longer an automatism stiffened in mimetic practices but a publicly recognized and validated ritual. Ritual, in its being a special act by definition, is performed for its symbolic meaning rather than as an action of ordinary life: this is what makes sociological play an extraordinary act in the ordinary and sometimes insignificant repetition of everyday life.

Ritual creates common feelings of group membership and moral obligations that require a certain kind of physical activity. To participate or not to participate in ritual is to further divide people into culturally distinct groups through symbolic stratification: First, the division opens between those who participate and those who do not. Sometimes a prescription not to participate is contemplated in the ritual itself. Examples, especially in rituals related to the distinction between pure and impure and male and female, are many and easily guessed (Douglas, 1966; Turner, 1969). The game reproduces these dynamics: on the one hand, it develops, as we have seen, from an implicit agreement on the message of initiation, whereby it distinguishes from the outset between those who are ready to play and those who are not—and the children who remain last in the middle of the field when choosing teammates before a ball game know this well; on the other hand, even within the game there are often prescriptions for isolation or suspension of the game itself. The decision to participate configures the beginning of the liturgy that distinguishes the ordinary, that brings out the significant element of human actions.

10.2. The Social Construction of Meaning

Play is a re-signification of ordinary activities. In light of play, such activities reoccur again, different, with other times and in other ways. They may be simple "non-serious" experiences but, crucially, culturally superior experiences to mundane reality. In their most socially meaningful nature, such experiences result in exclusion and inclusion. This can happen especially when play turns into sport. Sport, in fact, is a type of play that posits the competitive dimension (with others or with oneself) as the purpose of its very practice. Norbert Elias's in-depth study of sport as a process of civilization (Elias & Dunning, 1986) showed how the gradual decrease in physical violence marked the development of social organization capable of complex aggregations and functional relationships, thanks in part and above all to sport.

Far from yielding to a Decubertian sentimentality, Elias does not linger in listing the merits of sport as an inclusive occasion. There is no feel-good rhetoric in his dissection of the abreaction occasioned by sporting activity. Simply, man becomes better, more civilized, less barbaric, less sad, and less violent, if he can channel his passions and his wild destructive tension into a series of disciplined, coordinated, harmonious, and even beautiful and terrible practices—as beautiful and terrible as the heroes of the epic. How beautiful and terrible is the gesture of athletic perfection, the impossible balance on a gust of wind in the midst of a wave front on a surfboard, the half-clearance split of the center forward, the three-pointer of the shooting guard with seconds to go, the clatter of the sprinter's cleats, the scream of the weight thrower.

Elias would go so far as to say that sport, like civilization, risks degeneration, barbarization, if instead of the game we only care about the result. Today we would say, if instead of the game, one only cares about the profit in betting (hence the wicked tendency to cheat the same). Sport, like all elements of civilization, is fragile and ephemeral, the more it puts on the shoes of eternal enterprise. The alternative to sport is cheating, violence, and adulteration; the alternative to civilization is barbarism. So for Elias, but we might add a further step, namely a deep reflection on the meaning of play. Play is a kind of preparation for a range of activities that take place in society. By preparing one for the experience of acting and pretending, play teaches one to believe in the validity of social structures. Structures prescind from immediate subjective desires and the contingency of events; they represent their opposite pole. All this is because play is not individual expression but participation in an expressive act, whose meaning goes beyond the immediacy of the event and is linked to truths that transcend social action. The rules of play have in this an aesthetic dimension that is at one with religious ritual. To stop playing somehow also means to stop believing that there can be a dimension of existence that transcends existence itself. The ability to put social life into play is linked to the existence of a cultural dimension independent of individual identity and intimate desires and needs. The ability to be creative is greatly reduced if we crush the different levels of interaction on the plane of the monotony of a single, immediate reality. To stop playing is to lose a sense of the pliability of the world's reality. Sport, by exacerbating the staging of exclusion, simultaneously allows us to keep it under control, not to remove it. This, in a nutshell, we might say, is the meaning that is constructed together in play.

Play does not constitute a formula for solving social problems. The exclusion of the different—scapegoating—manifests itself in many ways, as many as the ways in which human beings dispose themselves to play. The possibility of all participating in the game, according to the rule of no one excluded, remains the ideal backdrop for an understanding of the mimetic nature of social relations, which trains itself daily in games, which reevaluates their meaning, which knows how to interrogate them and criticize them, even, when necessary. Denying that this quest continues basically means either taking refuge in an elitist utopianism of convenience—which is content with a select few who share the same ideals of peace, prosperity, and concord—or also entrenching oneself in exclusionary efficientism—which on the basis of abstract principles of meritocracy and ability refuses to recognize the social need of people on the margins. The awareness of the mimetic nature, which is acquired in play, on the other hand, is able to configure attention differently, without illusions, but also without fears.

To this lost, challenged, cynical, and monotonous world, sociological games are addressed. This is a sociology capable to play, a *playing sociology*.

References

Alberoni, F. (1977). *Movimento e istituzione*. Il Mulino.
Angiolino, A., Giuliano, L., & Sidoti, B. (2003). *Inventare i destini: I giochi di ruolo per l'educazione*. Edizioni la meridiana.
Antonello, P. P., & Gifford, P. (Eds.). (2015a). *Can we survive our origins? Readings in René Girard's theory of violence and the sacred*. Michigan State University Press.
Antonello, P. P., & Gifford, P. (2015b). *How we became human: Mimetic theory and the science of evolutionary origins*. Michigan State University Press.
Bataille, G. (1947). *La part maudit*. Les Editions de Minuit.
Bateson, G. (1972). *Steps to an ecology of mind*. Chandler.
Bauman, Z. (1995). *Life in fragments: Essays in postmodern morality*. Blackwell.
Bauman, Z. (2000). *Liquid modernity*. Blackwell.
Benasayag, M., & Schmit, C. (2003). *Les passions tristes: Soufferance psychique et crises sociale*. La Découverte.
Benveniste, E. (1947). Le jeu comme structure. *Deucalion*, 2, 161–167.
Benveniste, E. (1966). *Problèmes de linquistique* générale. Gallimard.
Berger, P., & Luckmann, T. (1995). *Modernität, pluralismus und sinnkrisis: Die orientierung des modernen Menschen*. Bertelsmann Stiftung.
Blumenberg, H. (1979). *Work on myth*. MIT Press.
Bondioli, A. (1996). *Gioco e educazione*. Franco Angeli.
Boockok, S.S., & Coleman, J. S. (1966). Games with simulated environments in learning. *Sociology of Education*, 39(3), 215–236.
Boockok, S. S., & Shild, E. O. (1968). *Simulation Games in Learning*. Sage.
Bourdieu, P. (1979). *Distinction: A social critique of the judgment of taste*. Harvard University Press.

Bowlby, J. (1969). *Attachment and loss: Vol 1. Attachment.* Basic Books.
Bruner, J. (1990). *Acts of meaning: Four lectures on mind and culture.* Harvard University Press.
Buber, M. (1923/2013). *I and thou.* Bloomsbury Publishing.
Caillois, R. (1958). *Les jeux et les hommes.* Gallimard.
Canetti, E. (1960). *Crowds and power.* Contimuum.
Capranico, S. (1997). *Role playing: Manuale a uso di formatori e insegnanti.* Raffaello Cortina.
Cartledge, P. (2006). *Thermopylae: The battle that changed the world.* Overlook.
Ceruti, M. (1986). *Constraints and possibilities.* Gordon and Breach.
Ciulla, J. B. (2020). Leadership and the power of resentment/ressentiment. *Leadership, 16*(1), 25–38.
Cohen, J. L. (2019). Populism and the politics of resentment. *Jus Cogens, 1*, 5–39.
Colllins, R. (1975). *Conflict sociology: Toward an explanatory science.* Free Press.
Cooley, C. H. (1902). *Human nature and social order.* Scribner.
Coser, L. A. (1956). *The functions of social conflict.* Free Press.
Crow, G. (2018). *What are community studies?.* Bloomsbury.
De Martino, E. (1977/2002). *La fine del mondo: Contributo all'analisi delle apocalissi culturali.* Einaudi.
Deleuze, G. (1968). *Différence et repetition.* Presses Universitaires de France.
Diamond, J. (2005). *Collapse: How societies choose to fail or succeed.* Viking.
Didi-Huberman, G. (1998). Vscosités et survivances. L'histoire de l'art à l'épreuve du matériau. *Critique, 54*(661), 138–162.
Douglas, M. (1966). *Purity and danger: An analysis of the concepts of pollution and taboo.* Routledge.
Dumouchel, P. (1995). *Emotions: Essai sur le corps et le social.* Synthélabo.
Dumouchel, P. (2015). *The barren sacrifice.* Michigan State University Press.
Dunkan, S., & Fiske, D. W. (1977). *Face-to-face interaction: Research methods and theory.* Erlbaum.
Dupuy, J. P. (1992). *Introduction aux sciences sociales: Logique des phénomenes collectifs.* Ellipses.
Dupuy, J. P. (2016). *La jalousie: Une géométrie du désir.* Seuil.
Dupuy, J.P., & Dumouchel, P. (1979). *L'énfer des choses: René Girard et la logique de l'économie.* Seuil.
Durkheim, E. (1912/1915). *The elementary forms of the religious life.* Allen & Unwin.
Eibl-Eibesfeldt, I. (1989). *Human ethology.* Gruyter.
Elias, N. (1933/1983). *The court society.* Pantheon.
Elias, N. (1969/2009). Sociology and psychiatry. In R. Kilminster & S. Mennell (Eds.), *The collected works of Norbert Elias: Essays III; On sociology and the humanities,* vol. 16 (pp. 159–179). University College Dublin Press.
Elias, N. (1978/2009). The concept of everyday life. In R. Kilminster & S. Mennell (Eds.), *The collected works of Norbert Elias: Essays III; On sociology and the humanities,* vol. 16 (pp. 127–134). University College Dublin Press.
Elias, N. (1991). *Mozart: Portrait of a genius.* Polity.
Elias, N., & Dunning, J. (1986). *Quest of excitement: Sport and leisure in the civilizing process.* Blackwell.
Falk, D. (2009). *Finding our tongues: Mothers, infants and the origins of language.* Gunstock Hill.

Fink, E. (1968). The oasis of happiness: Toward an ontology of play. *Yale Franch Studies, 41*, 19–30.
Foerster, H. von (1984). *Observing systems*. Intersystems.
Freud, S. (1911/2004). *The schreber case*. Penguin.
Freud, S. (1920/1955). *Beyond principle of pleasure*. Hogarth.
Fuller, S. (2006). *The new sociological imagination*. Sage.
Garfinkel, H. (1967). *Studies in ethnomethodology*. Polity.
Girard, R. (1978). *Violence and the sacred*. Johns Hopkins University Press.
Girard, R. (1982). *The scapegoat*. Johns Hopkins University Press.
Goffman, E. (1963). *Stigma: Notes on the management of the spoiled identity*. Prentice House.
Goffman, E. (1969). *Strategic interaction*. University of Pennsylvania Press.
Hadot, P. (2005). *Wittgenstein et les limits du langage*. Libraire Philosophique J. Vrin.
Hamilton, W. D. (1964). The genetical theory of social behavior. *Journal of Theoretical Biology, 7*(1), 1–52.
Huizinga, J. (1938/2002). *Homo ludens: A study of the play-element in culture*. Routledge.
Illich, I. (1976). *Medical nemesis: The expropriation of health*. Pantheon.
Kendon, A. (1988). Erving Goffman's approach to the study of face-to-face interaction. In A. Wootton & P. Drew (Eds.), *Erving Goffman: Exploring the interaction order* (pp. 14–40). Polity.
Lacan, J. (1975). *Le séminaire: Livre III. Les psychoses (1955–1956)*. Seuil.
Lacan, J. (1978). *Lacan in Italia / Lacan in Italie (1953–1978)*. La Salamandra.
Maturana, H. (1988). Ontology of observing: The biological foundations of self-consciousness and the physical domain of existence. In R. E. Donaldson (Ed.), *Texts in cybernetic theory: An in-depth exploration of the thought of Humberto Maturana, William T. Powers and Ernst von Glasersfeld* (pp. iv.1–iv.53). American Society of Cybernetics.
Mead, G. H. (1934). *Mind, self, and society*. University of Chicago Press.
Merton, R. K. (1949). *Social theory and social structure: Toward the codification of theory and research*. Free Press.
Mills, C. W. (1959). *The sociological imagination*. Grove Press.
Mishra, P. (2017). *Age of anger: A history of the present*. Farrar, Straus & Giroux.
Morin, E. (1973). *Le paradigme perdu: La nature humaine*. Seuil.
Moscovici, S. (1984). *Psychologie sociale*. Presses Universiataires de France.
Nancy, J. L. (1996). *Etre singulier pluriel*. Galilée.
Osborn, M. J., & Rubinstein, A. (1995). *A course in game theory*. MIT Press.
Pearce, B. W. (1989). *Communication and the human condition*. Southern Illinois University Press.
Piaget, J. (1975). *L'équilibration des structures cognitives: Problème central du développement*. Presses Universitaires de France.
Radin, P., Jung, C. G., & Kérényi, K. (1954/1972). *The trickster: A study in american indian mythology*. Schocken.
Riezler, K. (1941). Play and seriousness. *Journal of Philosophy, 38*(19), 505–517.
Ritzer, G. (2007). *The globalization of nothing*. Sage.
Sartre, J. P. (1947/1956). *Being and nothingness: A phenomenological essay on ontology*. Washington Square Press.
Schatzman, M. (1973). *Soul murder: Persecution in the family*. New American Library.

Sennett, R. (1976). *The fall of public man*. Knopf.
Sennett, R. (2008). *The craftsman*. Yale University Press.
Sennett, R. (2012). *Together: The rituals, pleasures, and politics of cooperation*. Yale University Press.
Simmel, G. (1901/1967). *The sociology*. Free Press.
Simonse, S. (2018). *Kings of disasters: Dualism, centralism and the scapegoat king in southeastern Sudan*. Michigan State University Press.
Sloterdijk, P. (2006). *Zorn und zeit: Politisch-psychologischer versuch*. Suhrkamp.
Smith, A. (1759/2006). *The theory of moral sentiments*. Meta Libri.
Sroufe, L. A. (1995). *Emotional development: The organization of emotional life in the early ages*. Cambridge University Press.
Stern, D. N. (1987). *The interpersonal world of the infant: A view from psychoanalysis and developmental psychology*. Basic Books.
Taylor, J., & Walford, R. (1972). *Simulation in the classroom: An introduction to role-play, games and simulation in education*. Penguin.
Thomas, W. I., & Thomas, D. S. (1928). *The child in america: Behavior problems and programs*. Knopf.
Tomelleri, S. (2009). *Identità e gerarchia: Per una sociologia del risentimento*. Carocci.
Tomelleri, S. (2015). *Ressentiment: Reflection on mimetic desire and society*. Michigan State University.
Tomelleri, S., & Doni, M. (2009). *Sociologie del sacro: Emozioni, credenze, miti e liturgie nelle scienze umane*. Morcelliana.
Turner, V. (1969). *The ritual processes: Structure and anti-structure*. Routledge.
Varela, F. (1979). *Principles of biological autonomy*. North Holland.
Watzlawick, P., Beavin, H., & Jakson, D. D. (1967). *Pragmatics of human communication: A study of interactional patterns, pathologies, and paradoxes*. Norton.
Webb, J. N. (2007). *Game theory: Decisions, interaction and evolution*. Springer.
Weil, S. (1956). *Cahiers: Tome 3*. Plon.
Winnicott, D. (1958). The capacity to be alone. In *The maturational processes and the facilitating environment: Studies in the theory of emotional development* (pp. 29–35). International Universities Press.
Winnicott, D. (1971). *Playing and reality*. Tavistock.
Wittgenstein, L. (1922/1969). *Tractatus logico-philosophicus*. Routledge.
Zamperini, A. (2007). *L'indifferenza: Conformismo del sentire e dissenso emozionale*. Einaudi.
Žižek, S. (1991). *For they know not what they do*. Verso.